Comments From Howard's Children

Dad has always been someone who exemplifies commitment to faith and to his family. Despite experiencing circumstances that might have challenged his faith he has continued to live a life that strives to draw people closer to Jesus Christ. One of the most important things that Dad has modeled throughout his life is the determination to never give up, despite what the situation looks like. His story offers inspiration and hope to everyone going through difficult times.

> - Jacqueline

Dad navigates two extremes that Christians commonly rush into. He doesn't put on a mask and pretend everything is all right when it's not, and he doesn't choose to wallow in self-pity, letting his situation contradict what the Bible teaches. He asks legitimate questions others have raised -even in scripture - and shares practical advice for working through those questions. He is an inspiration to all who know him.

> - Trevor

Although I see my father as highly educated, he displays an intriguing humility. I know his motive for writing this book is not for personal glory or edification, but rather to lend a helping hand to those who might find themselves in similar situations. He also desires to expand our own thinking to better empathize with those facing struggles, and to encourage us to help those in need. My father has been a tremendous encouragement to me, and the way he continues to cope with such an atrocious illness causes me to be even more inspired. I have never met a more righteous, honorable man, and it's a pleasure to call him my dad!

> - Shawn

Through it all, my Daddy is still my Daddy and the greatest man I've ever known. He has always been my rock, my constant and my strength. Throughout my life Dad taught me how to believe, how to have faith, how to hope and how to trust. Not only is he an incredible Father but also a genuine man of God who has influenced and inspired so many. His life of integrity, honor, truth and love has made it so easy for me to believe in a loving, faithful and true God.

> - Janine

Howard and his family would appreciate hearing what you have to share about this book. Let us know at valley@revtrev.com

WALKING THROUGH THE VALLEY

BY

Howard C. Lund dipTheo, BEd, MEd

Dealing with the Prospect of Death
With Bulbar A.L.S. (Lou Gehrig's Disease)

Walking Through the Valley – Dealing with the Prospect of Death With Bulbar A.L.S. (Lou Gehrig's Disease)

1st Edition October 2005

© Copyright 2005 by Howard C. Lund

Dedication

I would like to dedicate this book to my loving and faithful wife Ann and to our four children Jacqueline, Trevor, Shawn, Janine, and their families.

Ann my wife has been a fantastic support for me. I do believe God is going to reward her for the care and love that she has shown to me. She is very precious to me and I love her very much.

It thrills my heart to see each of our children and their families having a great desire to serve God with all their hearts, souls and minds. I believe my biggest contribution to this life will be coming through my God-fearing children. I believe that God has shown me that He will speak a blessing over our family that we have dedicated to Him. In Psalms 112:1-2 we read: "*Blessed is the man who fears the Lord who finds great delight in his commands. His children will be mighty in the land.*"

Due to my failing health our son Trevor has helped me in the final stages of this book to prepare it for publication. I do want to acknowledge him and thank him for all the work he has done.

My prayer for you is that as you read this book you will find out more about my loving and kind Heavenly Father who will never leave you no matter what valleys you go through. He is a God who will walk with you and when the time is very hard He will carry you through.

My hope is that when life's journey is over you will go to be with Him in heaven. As Revelation 21:11 states about heaven, "*It shone with the glory of God and its brilliance was like that of a very precious jewel, like a jasper, clear as crystal.*" Heaven is a wonderful place and my desire is that we will all spend it there together for eternity.

Table of Contents

Introduction   Page 11

Chapter One: *The Swift Progression of the Disease*   Page 15

Chapter Two: *My Personal Background*   Page 27

Chapter Three: *How God Has Been My Help*   Page 39

Chapter Four: *Questions I Have Had For God*   Page 53

Chapter Five: *The Difficulties with Adjustments*   Page 65

Chapter Six: *Faith versus Acceptance*   Page 79

Chapter Seven: *Personal Feelings Regarding My Condition*   Page 93

Chapter Eight: *Leaning on the Lord*   Page 107

Chapter Nine: *Living in Spiritual Victory*   Page 119

Chapter Ten: *The Future Glory All Believers Will Inherit*   Page 133

Chapter Eleven: *The Second Coming of Christ*   Page 149

Chapter Twelve: *An Update On My Condition*   Page 163

Chapter Thirteen: *Final Comments plus Caregiver's Thoughts*   Page 175

INTRODUCTION

I am in a rather interesting position so I have decided to write a book about what I am going through and how I am able to cope with the prospects of death. I am fifty – eight years old and have a potentially fatal illness that in the proper sense is known as "Bulbar ALS." Let me explain what this disease is so that you can understand where I am coming from. The bulbar form of Amyotrophic Lateral Sclerosis (also known as Lou Gehrig's Disease) has to do with the nerves in the back of my head (the Medulla Oblongata). The disease has caused the death of nerves in the bulbar region.

The result is that my throat and my mouth are severely affected. It is progressing very quickly, as I will discuss later. My swallowing is affected to the extent that I am now aspirating my saliva into my lungs. Therefore I am not eating food at the moment, but rather I am being fed with a tube into my stomach. My speech has also degenerated to the point that it is difficult for me to talk so that people can understand me. I therefore have a voice synthesizer that speaks for me after I type in the words that I want to say.

There is no cure for this disease. My life expectancy is not too good. With normal ALS, in which a person's arms and legs are affected, the life expectancy is considered to be about five years, although I have heard of cases in which people have lived much longer than that. With the Bulbar form of ALS, the life expectancy is less than five years. Some of the literature I have read suggests a life span from one to three years. I do know of cases where people have lived longer with this form of the disease as well. People with the regular form of A.L.S. usually get the Bulbar form towards the end of their lives. It is usually this form that takes their life.

A couple of the most common ways for patients to die with the form of the disease that has come upon me is through choking or by pneumonia. When the A.L.S. moves downward from the bulbar region, the next place it hits is quite often the lungs. If that happens, the victim simply starts to get very tired until equipment that helps him to breathe doesn't really help at all. He gets so tired that eventually he does not awaken from his sleep.

To date, I have experienced both of the first two problems. My last bout with pneumonia caused me to stay in the hospital for ten days, during which time I did some serious soul-searching and I made the decision that I might not have as much time to live as I thought I would. Therefore I knew that I would have to write this book as soon as possible to ensure that I have time to finish it. By the way, the third way of dying has struck home quite a bit as well. Even during the time that I was writing this book, my breathing has been a problem for me. You will see this further in the book where I am giving updates on my condition.

With this book I hope to be of assistance to others who walk through terminal diseases. Such a disease makes us think very seriously about the future. At the same time, we can feel very lonely. If this book can be a help to such people, then I will be very satisfied. My heart goes out to others who have been afflicted with such, because I know where you are coming from, and I want to help you in this process.

It could be that I could help caregivers for this book as well. I have a very strong circle of support, but I realize that some going through similar situations might not. My wife has been my strongest caregiver, and she will be giving some of her observations in the last chapter of this book. My wife's name is Ann and we have been married for about thirty-eight years. I also want to point out to you my strongest level of support that gives me hope where there otherwise is no hope. That level of hope comes from God. In this way I might give you some hope regardless of your condition.

I should explain why I chose this title for my book. Most of us would have heard somewhat of Psalm 23 in the Bible, which is known as the Shepherd's Psalm. I have included a verse from it here: *"Even though I walk through the valley of the shadow of death, I will fear no evil, for You are with me; Your rod and Your staff, they comfort me"* (Ps. 23:4). Walking through a fatal disease, I thought this is an appropriate title. I am currently "walking through the valley of the shadow of death." By the way, as the psalmist stated, I also "will fear no evil." So this is where I get the title.

This book will be largely autobiographical in context so that you will understand where I am coming from. I have rarely spent much time talking about myself but I feel this could be helpful to others who are going through similar circumstances. I will relate my background to this book. In talking about such things as my family and when I discuss how various doctors and nurses have been and assistance to me you will see that I am blessed with a tremendous system of support. Hopefully each one who is walking through a fatal disease is receiving a similar level to help in their journey.

My real focus though, is not on me but upon God who has been my help through this entire ordeal. It is God who has been my strength and I want to give Him praise for that. He is my real source of strength. I pray that He might bless you as you read this book, and that you may feel inspired by it.

Chapter One:

The Swift Progression of the Disease

The experts say that no two cases for people with A.L.S. are the same. It turns out that whoever has this disease has a unique variety of it, with symptoms that are different from others. Even the end result might be different – some will live longer than others.

First Symptoms

The first symptoms I felt were in December of 2003. At the time I was Principal of Prairie Junior/Senior High in Three Hills, Alberta. I was basically preparing the school to become an Alternate School within a public system that is known as Golden Hills School Division. That December while lying on my back one night, I felt something strange in my throat. Something seemed to lie flat against the back of my throat. It meant that I could not lie on my back for long periods of time. It was awkward for me to do so.

That February I went to see a doctor for the first time in Three Hills. He wanted to give me a complete physical. Being very thorough, he had the lab conduct several tests. The results were that I was in good physical condition. I asked him to check with my throat to see if there was anything wrong there. After checking he felt that everything was normal.

The Beginning of Tests

I kept up a pretty hectic schedule at work, because in order to meet the requirements of Golden Hills, we had to release several staff members. It was a very difficult time, because we had very good people working for us. However, my condition continued to deteriorate even though my time was very busy.

At a granddaughter's birthday party in Edmonton during the month of March, a doctor friend who was there thought that I had received a stroke because my speech was becoming slurred. Then in April, I came home from work with slurred speech and Ann wondered as well if it wasn't a stroke. As a result we decided to see our family doctor back in Edmonton where we had lived for a number of years. We saw him on Monday of our Spring Break. He checked me over very carefully and told me that he wanted me to see a specialist. He said that he would arrange this for me. Thinking that this would take several weeks, we left home to visit family members because we were on Spring Break. By Thursday of that week he had gotten in touch with me to tell me that I should go to the Emergency at the University Hospital in Edmonton on Friday morning, telling the receptionist of the suspicion that my malady might be bulbar palsy and that I needed to see a neurologist. I had no idea what bulbar palsy was at the time (it is another name for bulbar ALS) but this didn't sound good.

I spent the day at the Emergency, getting checked over by interns, residents, and other doctors. Finally the neurologist on call, Dr. Siddiqi, came to see me. He gave me the same tests for stroke that the other doctors had, telling us that that would be the best option for me. That night he arranged for me to have a CAT scan and the results showed normal - it did not appear to be a stroke. However, he said that the affliction could not be diagnosed until a lot of tests were done to eliminate other possibilities. He would arrange for me to have those tests. An application form was filled out for me to have an MRI done.

It was interesting that the reason given to have an MRI done was to check for pseudo bulbar palsy, which is a variation of the regular bulbar palsy. In the case of pseudo bulbar palsy, the nerves affected are higher up in the brain than for standard bulbar palsy. I had, and still have, one of the symptoms of pseudo bulbar palsy, and that relates to emotions. People with pseudo bulbar palsy have fits of crying and laughter at times when laughter or crying really isn't suitable. I didn't get the emotion of laughter but I certainly have the emotion for crying. If I am watching something that is rather touching, I begin crying quickly. If my family members are doing something that is really good, I end up in tears. It has been a frustrating emotion at times, and while there is medication to control that, I am not on it.

We went back to Three Hills so I could resume my responsibilities there. Very soon we got a phone call stating that an MRI was scheduled for me the next Thursday morning and that Dr. Siddiqi wanted to see me that afternoon. Therefore we drove to Edmonton on Wednesday evening and were at the University Hospital at 8:00 A.M. Thursday for the MRI. That afternoon we went to see Dr. Siddiqi and he had scheduled me for tests that afternoon. I was checked over again by resident doctors to see what my symptoms were and then I was given tests to check on my nerve reactions as well as an EMG to check on how my muscles were doing.

The test for nerves involved electrodes being put over nerves on one side of my body. When the electric current hit, the reaction was good as far as I know. The EMG involved putting needles into my muscles. Again, this showed that my muscles in my arms and legs were doing well. The final thing Dr. Siddiqi did was to put a needle into my tongue. This was a very painful exercise, but it demonstrated that I had weaknesses there. It was evident that there was damage to those nerves leading to my tongue.

That evening Dr. Siddiqi arranged for me to have a swallowing test done including a fluoroscopy, which takes an x-ray video of a person swallowing foods that are laced with barium. In the morning the staff from the Glenrose Hospital phoned to schedule the test. I was given food to eat while a team of three watched my swallowing. These involved a speech pathologist, an occupational therapist, and a nutritionist.

After that assessment we were taken underground to the Royal Alexandra Hospital where I had the fluoroscopy. Later my wife and I were permitted to see the video, which showed that there was a location in my throat where food stayed for awhile. The danger was that it could go the wrong way, possibly causing choking. It was suggested that I swallow everything a couple of times to clear that area out. The results were that "trace elements" might be going into my lungs.

I was quite overwhelmed by the flurry of tests that were arranged for me. Usually many of these tests are given over a few months. Both an MRI and a fluoroscopy are normally expected to take a couple of months to book. I had both these tests within one week (including the CAT scan). This demonstrated to me the seriousness of things.

Dr. Siddiqi then said that there probably would not be any more tests for about four months, because they had to see how the disease would progress. Obviously there was the thought that it might move into my arms and legs as well. Therefore we returned to our home in Three Hills with a suspicion of what it was, but with no definite diagnosis.

My family very quickly looked up the disease on the Internet and found that the prognosis was not good for me. They did not want me to do the same research but eventually I did so anyway. My wife Ann and I discussed the ramifications and the prospects for the future.

In July we moved back to Edmonton to be near the doctors. I had two choking episodes before June that scared Ann a great deal. Also my speech was noticeably getting a lot worse. My arms and legs are as good as ever, which I am very thankful for.

However, I knew that I could not work outside the home any longer because of my difficulty with speaking. I also had to be very careful in eating, cutting my food up into very small pieces and chewing them up a great deal. It meant that I was now taking twice as long in eating my food as others would take. Ann had to be very patient with me because she was often finished long before I was.

Developments from April to August

In August we had another meeting with Dr. Siddiqi. We gave him a sheet showing how the disease had developed since we last had met with him in April. I am including that material here:[1]

1. There is a weakness developing in my jaws. I am yawning much more with this condition, and when I yawn, at least one of my jaws usually pop (at the joints of the jaws). This happens more on the right side.

2. Developments in my mouth are quite extensive. It seems that saliva comes more to the front of my mouth. I can feel thirsty at the back of my mouth when I have saliva at the front.

    •   My lips are much weaker, and once in a while saliva will come out of my mouth (drooling).

    •   I have less control of my tongue.

    •   I am chewing my food much more. It takes me about twice as long to eat a meal. Food also gets stuck in my mouth and in my teeth more. I cannot always clean out my mouth with my tongue. I have to use my finger to clean the food from the side of my mouth. I haven't cut down on amounts of food yet.

    •   I am trying to take smaller sips of liquids, but when I forget, fluids sometimes come shooting out of my mouth and over my front, etc.

---

[1] "Developments Since the April Appointments"

- Cheeks, especially on the left side, often end up between my teeth. However, I can end up chewing the inside of my lip (on the left side) when I eat. If I lie on my left side and talk (e.g. in bed), I can end up with my cheek between my teeth. I have found that I have been chewing using the front of my mouth, and thereby chewing my lip. When I chew from the teeth at the back of my mouth, I don't chew my lip.

- My tongue gets bitten once in awhile (more on the edges) but harder sometimes when I sneeze.

3. My nose has been doing some strange things as well.

   - I sometimes have difficulty blowing my nose. My throat gets involved.

   - I generally have much less matter in my nose (in fact, my nose is often quite dry).

   - My nose can seem to be plugged up with nothing there. On some mornings, my nose can seem so plugged up that I cannot breathe out of it (when lying on my right side). If I turn over on my left side, I can breathe easily, with very little impediment in my nose.

   - When I wipe the inside of my nose with a Kleenex, my nose seems more plugged up than before.

4. My speech has really been changed, so that it is sometimes difficult for me to talk (especially if I haven't talked much during the day). It is slurred.

   - People are now regularly asking me what I have said. That has developed more in the last two months.

   - I am scheduled to begin speech therapy tomorrow (August 17) at the Grey Nuns Hospital.

5. My emotions are a problem, especially crying. This seems to be more frequent now.

6. I have a lot of mucous in my mouth at times, especially when I go to bed.

7. I cannot lie on my back for very long, because the soft palate seems to lie down, giving me an uncomfortable feeling in my throat.

When Dr. Siddiqi saw the information that I gave him, he underlined almost everything that I had written down. These were consistent with bulbar palsy. After checking me over some more, he was ready to give me the diagnosis. He confirmed that it was bulbar palsy, which he said for the first time, was considered to be part of A.L.S. He also gave me the sobering facts, saying that with regular A.L.S. the life expectancy is five years, but with my form of it, the life expectancy is less than five years.

Further Developments until Present Time

After August, my condition continued to deteriorate quite quickly. I had to make some adaptations. Also during this time we became acquainted with other resources that were available to help me.

Help Needed For Speaking

In August I went to an appointment at the Grey Nuns Hospital where my speech was being tested. A battery of tests were given to me and in a few weeks we were called back to go over the results. It was found that at that time people could understand 80% of what I said. This was good news, but it didn't last too long. My speech was regressing quite quickly.

As time went by and because of the prospects involved with my ability to speak, I was becoming quite frustrated. I could no longer clearly say what I wanted to, and close family members now had to ask me what I said. This was quite a problem for me that did not have any promise of getting better. I was not really ready to give up talking, but I knew that the time might be coming.

We were referred by the speech pathologist at the Grey Nuns to the ICAN Center, which is at the Glenrose Hospital. There we were introduced to some talking devices and asked which one I might like to use. The voice synthesizer that seemed the most suitable for me was the "Link" machine. We obtained that in the middle of November (free of charge). I still did not use it too much because it was more of a novelty. I was able to function reasonably well though people were having a hard time to understand me.

However, by January my speech had regressed to the point where I use the voice synthesizer almost all of the time in talking to various people. I have to even use it when talking to Ann on various occasions, though she can understand me better than anyone else can.

Help Needed With My Swallowing

My regression did not end with my speech. In the middle of September we went to the Grey Nuns so that I could have another swallowing test to see if I was aspirating any food into my lungs. There was no sign of aspiration at that time and I was pretty happy about that.

In October I had another episode with choking that I was able to clear up myself. I decided at that point I could no longer have the skin of baked potatoes because that was the culprit for me. My ability to swallow seemed to be going downhill very quickly.

I had been eating foods carefully, regularly using small bites and chewing them up. In December, however, I choked twice on small chunks of food. I had to be given the Heimlich maneuver, once by my son, and once by a total stranger in California. We think he might have been an angel, but we are not sure that is literally the case.

This meant that changes had to be made as my condition continued to worsen. It involved two stays in the hospital and meant that I would have to give up eating foods.

Challenges with Pneumonia

Early in December, I developed a bad cough. Dr. Siddiqi told me to get to Emergency as soon as possible. While a bad cough would not hospitalize normal people, it was dangerous for people with this disease. I went to the hospital and stayed there for four days.

During that time I was given minced food and it was suggested that I should be eating similar food at home. I met the head of the Neurological Department who was familiar with ALS. I also met Dr. Kalra, who works with the A.L.S. Clinic. It was Dr. Kalra who discharged me from the hospital and gave me medication that was designed to cut down the amount of saliva I was getting into my mouth.

Soon after I was discharged from the hospital, we had an appointment to go see Dr. Siddiqi who said that the disease was progressing very quickly and that steps had to be taken to help me live longer. He felt that I was aspirating my saliva and that is why I had a chest infection that turned out to be pneumonia. He stated that he would arrange for a food tube to be put into my stomach so that I would not be eating foods through my mouth any longer.

We were going to go with the entire family to California to see our oldest son, Trevor, and his family off as they were moving to New Zealand. I was on antibiotics constantly, and when we got home we purchased a food processor so my food could be totally blended. The trip was a good one, but because I was severely limited with what I could eat I lost about six pounds.

The pneumonia was not totally gone. After I was off the medication, I almost immediately began to once again develop a severe cough. When a respiratory therapist visited our home she felt that I should go to the hospital very soon. My faithful general practitioner (Dr. Myrholm) checked me over in our home and said that I needed to go to Emergency that evening. During that night in Emergency at the University Hospital it was determined that it was a severe lung infection (probably pneumonia) and that I needed to be admitted into the hospital as soon as possible. Before 8:00 A.M. I was moved to the Medicine Department and treatment was started immediately. Something was going to take place that would change my perspective on life completely.

Staring Death Face to Face

While my pneumonia (which was very serious) was starting to break up, I still had a very severe cough. But doctors applauded. It was needed to get the phlegm out of my lungs. On January 27 while in hospital I wrote the following in my voice synthesizer so that I would have these thoughts to record later:

> I would like to talk about my condition. I have been in the hospital since Sunday night and it is now Thursday. In talking to the Nutritionist, I will probably be here until next Monday, January 21 (it turned out to be Tuesday, Feb. 1). I have been very sick with what is both pneumonia and bronchitis. I hope that I can get this cured so that I don't get a repetition of this again. I think that what I had in December was not really cured. This

time I became very concerned because I think this is probably the way I will eventually die. I have been brought face to face with the possibility of death during this time in the hospital. I basically choked on phlegm. I had coughed up a great deal of phlegm which filled a good part of my mouth. It took me about twenty minutes to get all the phlegm cleared out. I fully realized what it means to die by choking on your own phlegm. It was a very stressful time for me as well, and I am sure that it was a great strain on my heart as well so I can see how I could have a heart attack during such an occasion. It is ironic that I had another occasion in which I am sure I could have brought up another big bunch of phlegm. However I deliberately didn't do that, because I felt it would have been dangerous to do so. I don't want to lose my life choking on phlegm just yet. This really made me do some serious thinking. My life might not last as long as I originally thought when I got this disease. Therefore I had to make plans to get the book about my condition written as soon as possible.[2]

Coming face to face with death is a very sobering experience. Since I have been working at home since last August, I was writing another book that the Lord had put on my heart several years ago. I am almost three-quarters of the way finished with that book but I have put it to the side until I finish writing this one. My experience tells me that my life might not be too much longer and I feel very compelled to put this to a pen before my life is gone.

A PEG Installed in My Stomach

During the hospital stay I had a PEG (a feeding tube) inserted in my stomach through an operation. It included a great deal of training so that now at home I can feed myself with no problems. Also all medications that I take have to be in liquid form so that I can inject them into my stomach with a syringe.

At first, I really did not want to have a feeding tube installed. I knew that would mean that I could no longer eat regular foods. However, to be perfectly honest, the feeding tube probably added several years to my life (at least I hope so). It is interesting that before I went into the hospital, I was considered to be under the Palliative Care section

---

[2] "Thoughts Regarding a Fatal Disease", page 33

of the Home Care department. After I came out with the tube, it was changed to the general care instead. It does not usually happen that way!

The PEG did make a difference in my life, and hopefully I will not die with pneumonia in the future. This can happen if I am not taking in food through my mouth. Now, however, I am under the Long Time Care department.

This has been quite an experience for me. Probably the greatest problem is that I can no longer eat food, and our society is set up in such a way that you see food commercials on TV regularly. But it also means an end to going to restaurants for dining out. There are specific hours in which you have to be home to feed yourself. It also means a change in the way your body operates. With regular food, I very rarely was constipated, but now it is a common occurrence. I expect to solve this once I can start getting more exercise

Solving Saliva Problems

The official diagnosis of my pneumonia was called "aspiration pneumonia." In other words, I got the pneumonia by aspirating my own saliva into my lungs. Apparently surplus saliva can go into my lungs without me knowing about it. Once there, it causes the infections that I have had. Because of this factor I felt compelled to reduce the amount of saliva in my mouth significantly so that I will not be aspirating any more.

It is important to understand that people with this sickness do not get any more saliva than people regularly get. The problem is that I don't swallow my saliva as normal people do. It is impossible. I am able to swallow the saliva that is in my mouth, which is greatly reduced because of medication.

There is another problem that arises because I don't eat food through my mouth. It has become tremendously important for me to brush my teeth about four times a day and to rinse my mouth with a medicated mouthwash in order to keep my mouth clean and healthy. I even brush my tongue on a regular basis.

Right from the beginning I had a white tongue, which is called a "furry tongue"[3] by the A.L.S. Manual. I cleared my tongue up by brushing it four times a day, and applying the mouthwash on it the same

---

[3] "Living With ALS", page 57

number of times. Mouth hygiene is now of greatly increased importance. I have to try to keep my saliva clean.

Medical Practitioners That Have Been of Assistance

I have had a myriad of health practitioners. They have been extremely helpful for me. My own personal family doctor, Dr. Myrholm, has been tremendously helpful. The specialists, including Dr. Siddiqi, have also been of invaluable assistance to me. I have had the help of speech pathologists, occupational therapists, respiratory specialists, and other specialized nurses.

The medical community has been of great help and support, and I thank God for them. I am now part of the A.L.S. Society and they also have offered a tremendous amount of help, including an electronic bed, which rises for me (I have to sleep with the head of my bed raised). The A.L.S. Clinic, which I will be attending, offers the help of several medical people who are specialized to deal with my condition.

What Lies Ahead?

In writing this chapter I have not included all the details. For example, I found that if I laid on my right side I could not breathe through my left nostril of my nose. I asked doctors about it and they did not know the answer. However, when I read material that I got from the A.L.S. office, I found that this condition occurs due to "weakness of the muscles which normally elevate the nostrils and open the airways."[4] The cure for it was to get "Breathe Right" tape, which is used by athletes, and put that across my nose at night. It works very well.

Even as I write this book I am not sure of how much time I have left. If I come down with pneumonia once more it could be "game over." Therefore I am doing everything I can to ensure that my lungs stay clear. Even after I left the hospital I got another infection in my lung. However I had the medication on hand to use and it got cleared up very soon. My main task now is to control my saliva. I have the medication to do that.

The other question that has been surfacing is: when is God going to heal me? Several (including non-Christians) have had dreams of me

---

[4] "Living With ALS," page 19

speaking normally. I feel that God could very well heal me. If He does such a thing, I would spend the rest of my days (as I will anyway) pointing others to the great God that we serve, and the great Healer who can heal any disease. Perhaps by the time I finish writing this book I will be healed! May God bless you as you read further information about my life and the choices I have made.

Chapter Two:

My Personal Background

I felt that it was important for me to tell you something of my background so that you would understand where I am coming from and the kind of support that I have. I have been blessed in many ways, for which I thank God.

My Childhood and Teenage Years

I was born and raised in Central Alberta, Canada. I was raised on a farm and so the occupation that I became used to was milking cows, cultivating soil, haying, and harvesting – the events that most farmers are involved in. I attended school in a small hamlet near our farm and then I was bussed to Red Deer for the last two grades. As far as my schooling was concerned I made sure that I took the right courses that would allow me eventually to go to University, though that wasn't in my plans at the time.

There were some very important and difficult events that took place in my childhood and teenage years. When I was only ten years old my mother Sylvia was hospitalized with kidney infection. The day before she was to come home from the hospital the disease progressed to the point that the kidneys failed and were poisoning her system.

She passed away at the young age of forty-five. I recall that day very well. I remember after hearing the news of my mother's condition I went running out to the trap lines where I knew that my brother Ralph was so I could give him the news. We both went running as fast as we possibly could back to the farmhouse. When we arrived at our home no one was there. Everyone had gone to the hospital and left us there alone. What a feeling of despair and loneliness came upon me.

This was quite a tragedy for us because our mother was the head of our household. I can hardly remember my father ever being around. In order to bring income in for our family he was working a long way from home. My oldest sister Helen was married at the time so she took my younger sister Darlene to live with her. My oldest brother Ray was then left to look after Ron, Ralph and myself. My brother Eino was working away from home at the time of Mom's passing and soon after my brother Ron also went out working.

Six years later my oldest brother Ray who was now already married and had his first daughter, Brenda, took his wife Annie into the hospital to have their second child, Brian. Ray returned home that night and went to sleep. When morning came my younger sister Darlene arose from her sleep to find our brother Ray dead on the floor. He had a severe diabetic seizure during the night and it took his life at twenty-nine.

I had just gone to Calgary to look for work. My life was once again changed and I returned home to help out around the farm. But there were two very positive events that took place while I was a teenager that changed my life even more.

The first event took place before my brother passed away. It was the fact that I found Jesus Christ as my Saviour in a church in Sylvan Lake. When I started being bussed to Red Deer, I met a friend on the bus who soon invited me to the Youth Group meetings at the church, which I gladly attended. At the time I felt I needed friends and the Youth Group was a good place to find them. Soon I began going to church on Sundays with them and it wasn't long after that that I found Christ as my Saviour. I was sixteen years old at that time. No one else in my family attended church regularly.

The second great event that took place was at a Camp meeting later on in the summer – this was a Camp meeting that I wouldn't have been at if my brother had not died. While God blessed me in remarkable ways at the Camp, I was also blessed to be introduced to a girl who would eventually become my wife. Ann was very special to me right from the start, and I was encouraged to get to know her family, who were also very special. After visiting her several times, we grew to love each other and were eventually married in 1967. Ann has been very special in my life ever since, especially after I came down with the disease I now face.

Generally my childhood and my teen years were very good years in my life. I so much enjoyed the farm life that I had. The wide open spaces were important for me, and often I would go for walks around the farm. However, I was also very thrilled when the time came to leave home and start my post – secondary training. I did not know what that training would mean for me, but I really wanted to follow God's direction in my life right from the start.

My Post Secondary Training

I knew that post-secondary education was going to be very important in my life, even though few of my family members were involved in it. There was an important event, which happened while I was still on the farm that indicated where I should go first for my training.

At home we had dairy cattle and I had to milk before going to school or doing other activities. With no running water in our house, we had a reservoir in the stove that had hot water in it. One morning I was in a hurry so I was going to wash up with cold water. However, God spoke to my heart very clearly, asking me if that was the way I was going to treat Him.

I knew He asked that if I was going to wash with cold water, was I going to be lukewarm or cold towards Him? The truth struck home very quickly. Needless to say, I washed with hot water! This event has been my motivating factor throughout my life. I have always tried to be zealous for God.

I started nine years of post-secondary training by attending Northwest Bible College in Edmonton, Alberta (now called Vanguard Bible College). This was useful for preparing me for ministry and after three years I could have stepped into ministry.

It is interesting that while Bible College can prepare you for ministry it is God who teaches you to pray and to be in constant communion with Him. This was a tremendous time, because I learned the Bible much better and experienced the three Persons of the Godhead much closer (the Father, Son, and Holy Spirit). In those years the Bible School emphasized the need for prayer and perseverance.

Ann and I were married between my second and third years, so we had the adjustment to married life as well. Ann was one of the wives who were given a "PHT" pin (Putting Hubby Through) at the graduation banquet. She had worked in a hospital in the nursing field to help us make ends meet. That wasn't the only time she did that.

I had more training ahead of me. I felt that in order to pastor a small church I would need another trade that would be useful for supplementing our income. From the Bible College I earned a three-year diploma in theology. That was only the beginning of the training that God had for me.

After graduating from Bible College, I began to take University courses at Camrose Lutheran College (now called Augustana University College). From there I was able to get two years of teacher training. I then transferred to the University of Alberta for the third year of training, with the intention of beginning to teach school after that. At that time this was allowable for those who took a three-year program. Our first daughter, Jacqueline, was born to us and we felt that God was blessing us in giving us a family.

During that time I also had been involved in a pastoral ministry. A classmate of mine pastored the Nazarene Church in Camrose. However, he left to pursue other activities, and he recommended to his church that I become interim pastor there while they looked for a replacement.

The summer before I began my third year of University, I pastored at the Nazarene Church. It turned out that they liked me and did not look for anyone else. I ended up pastoring there for about one year, and finally had to tell them that I had to leave because I was going to start teaching school. They then obtained a new pastor.

After I completed my third year of University, I sent out applications for beginning my career as a teacher. God gave me a position in the Wetaskiwin County jurisdiction. While I was teaching there, my training did not stop. Every summer I went back to University to take my fourth year of training. At the end of three summers, I graduated from the University and gained my Bachelor's Degree in Education.

About fifteen years later while I was pastoring (I'll give you more information about that soon), I felt led by God to take some more training in the education field. By this time, I had been principal of a school in the Wetaskiwin County as well as being the founding principal of two private schools.

After pastoring and substitute teaching, etc. for seven years, I decided that it would be good to obtain more education. In 1986 I enrolled in the University of Alberta Graduate Program, working on a Master's Degree in Educational Administration. I had been an administrator for a number of years. I did not know what doors the Lord might open in the future but He seemed to be leading me in this way. It turned out that with teaching assistantships and student teacher consultant positions, my degree ended up costing me very little.

As you might guess, I have loved to take training throughout my life. As God opened doors for me to do so, I stepped through. I have felt that in God's plans for me, there was a very real purpose for advanced training. In total then, I have taken nine years of post-secondary training. I thank God for his presence, guidance and for helping me to learn what He deemed was important for His purpose.

My Teaching and Administrative Careers

I began my teaching career at Lakedell School in the County of Wetaskiwin. This was a very nice position where I got to know what teaching involved and I also got to know several people. When the principal was away, I became acting principal.

I taught there for about two years and seven months. Our second child was born, this time a son, whom we named Trevor. Early in the year of 1974, the Assistant Superintendent of the County approached me. He was our neighbor and he suggested that I apply for a principalship for a school in the extreme eastern section of the County. Though I had not thought of administration before, this seemed to be an open door that the Lord was leading me into. After the ensuing interviews, I was accepted as principal of Rosebrier School. I began work there in April of that year.

Rosebrier School was a very unique situation. It was a very small school. It went from Grade One to Grade Nine and there had to be at least two grades for each class. We had four teachers so one teacher had to teach three grades at a time. This was an interesting learning situation for me because I had to be administrator as well as a teacher. We generally took turns in teaching three classes at once. I did accept that challenge as well, and it didn't worked out too badly.

The situation was not too bad because this was a very good community, where most parents had deep spiritual roots. Parents were generally very supportive and not many students misbehaved. We enjoyed this time very much because of the friendly environment that we were in. We felt blessed by God.

Each Sunday we would travel to Camrose for Church. Camrose was about a half an hour away (we had been traveling to Camrose even when I was working at Lakedell School which was an hour away).

It was during our stay at Rosebrier our third child and second son, Shawn, was born in Camrose. We now had three charming children and we were a very happy family.

Another administrative position came open in Calgary. A new church wanted to have a private Christian school opened. I was asked to become the founding principal and, after much prayer and discussion with my wife, I accepted that position. I felt that God was leading us to this ministry, so we left my comfortable job behind to begin a new work for Him.

I became the founding principal of Foothills Christian Academy that after several years has now been merged with Heritage Christian School in Calgary. It was interesting to start a school from scratch, and there were many parents who shared the vision of education in a Christian setting for their children. However, after being there for a short time we definitely felt that God was calling us again – this time for a pastoral ministry.

It was also during this time that our fourth and last child was born. Our youngest daughter, Janine, was born at Grace Hospital in Calgary. Ironically this was the same hospital that Ann had been born in.

While Janine was born in Calgary, most of her days growing up would be in another setting - not as a principal's daughter but as a pastor's daughter. It would mean a move away from a city back to a rural setting a few miles out of Thorsby, Alberta.

I would now be teaching something else - the Word of God to a small church congregation where Christ would be exalted and glorified. When I had been involved as a principal of a private Christian school, I had felt that this was an important ministry for me. However, the ministry that God was now calling me to seemed to be very important as well.

I should point out that my years as a school administrator were not over yet, because God would show me in the future other schools that He wanted me to become involved in. However, for now His call in my heart would be for a pastoral setting. Being in a small church, I would have to supplement my income by substitute teaching. I would do this for quite awhile during the time I was a pastor.

Entering Full Time Pastoral Ministry

We approached the Superintendent of the Alberta District of the Pentecostal Assemblies of Canada for a ministry license and to see if any churches were open at that time. It wasn't long after I received my credentials that a church called us, asking us to come and preach for a call. It was a small church in Thorsby, Alberta (twenty-two miles west of Leduc). We were accepted there and I would be preaching twice each Sunday as well as leading a Bible Study every Wednesday evening. I also led the Youth services for part of the time that we were there. My ministry went very well, and we soon gained the respect of our congregation.

In 1981 I was officially ordained as a pastor for the Pentecostal Assemblies of Canada in October. I asked for and was granted to be ordained in the church I was pastoring. It was a highlight because good friends of ours also attended the service.

We did see God move in wonderful ways during our time in Thorsby. Each Sunday night we had an altar service and for many of those times, our children came forward to seek God. I am sure that was important to them in their desire to become servants of God in the future. Many others also had their lives changed at that time. God really blessed all who came to Him.

We also had a prayer time during each morning service for those who had needs. We saw God perform several miracles for people as they reached out in faith for God to meet their needs. We still praise God for verifying our ministry there!

It was also a precious time for leading people to the Lord. One family that comes to mind was a family that lived on the road on the way to the house where our children were taking music lessons. Since I didn't have anything to do during the weekly sessions, I would go and visit the family up the road. Eventually the entire family came to know the Lord!

God was very good at ensuring that our services had His presence with us as well as His power. Pastoring was generally a very positive experience for us, even though I had a tendency of getting very busy with other responsibilities.

I feel that administration was one of my strongest gifts for the church, although I was well aware of other gifts that He had given me to minister to His people. God truly blessed us when we were there. We were very grateful to Him for that.

Supplementing My Pastoral Salary

When I began to substitute teach within the County of Leduc (as it was then called) it was a big help for me to get to know several teachers particularly in the west end of the school jurisdiction. God had been very faithful to us by providing for us when we were very low on income and He continued after He called me to become a vocational pastor.

Substitute teaching was very useful to me then because it fit in well with my ministry. I received three temporary teaching contracts while substitute teaching in that jurisdiction. God demonstrated His faithfulness to us once again!

While I was in Thorsby, I was also asked to be the founding principal of another private Christian School. A friend of mine was pastoring the church in Leduc and though it was a very busy time for me to be a full-time principal as well as a full-time pastor, I agreed to do this temporarily - just to get the school started. I became the founding principal of Leduc Christian Academy, and served that school for one year.

I also felt that God wanted me to go back to University during this time and gain a Master's Degree. As I mentioned earlier, I did not know what I would be doing with a Master's Degree, but the doors seemed to open for me to pursue it. After I had obtained my degree, I was able to use my training while I was still pastoring.

Uses of My Master's Degree While Still Pastoring

Soon after I finished my degree, I was asked to conduct a study on the level of satisfaction people had in the town of Calmar and area (Calmar was a few miles east of where we lived). This used the same type of parameters that my thesis did, which explored the level of teacher satisfaction in the two rural jurisdictions that I had been teaching in - Wetaskiwin and Leduc. For the Calmar study, a survey was conducted of students, adults, and seniors. This was done for a countywide agency known as the F.C.S.S. in the County of Leduc. Because of my University contacts, I was able to have the same lady at the University put the results through the computer program and tabulate them for me. The results were very interesting and caused some dramatic changes to be made in the town of Calmar.

One year later I asked to do the same study for Thorsby and District, except that this study would involve everyone and not just a sample as Calmar's did. The result was that there was a lot more material to be tabulated. Change in the Thorsby area was not as needful as in the Calmar area, and many responses were significantly different from that found in the Calmar study. The final report for each of these studies was well over one hundred pages.

Once I received my Master's Degree I did very little substitute teaching any longer. My focus was more upon adult students. Very soon I was recommended by the principal of Thorsby High School to teach for what was then known as Alberta Vocational College (now Nor'Quest College). I started teaching part-time at the Pembina Consortium in Drayton Valley, and later taught at the main campus in downtown Edmonton on a part-time basis. At the same time, I began teaching part-time as an adjunct faculty member at what was then Northwest Bible College, the same school I attended many years previously.

This was a very busy time for me because it involved a lot of traveling to get to my work. After 15 years of pastoring we felt that God was leading us in a different direction and it was time to once again make a change in our lives. So I resigned as Pastor and we moved into Edmonton.

When I started my career in the classroom and as a school administrator (soon afterwards), God was planning for me to finish my public career in the way that I started it – in a school. After a few months of rest, God then opened the door for me to become principal of Millwoods Christian School in south Edmonton. As well as providing leadership for the school, God gave me a vision of something greater for its future.

My Role as Principal of Millwoods Christian School

As principal of Millwoods Christian School, my training for two occupations came into full view. As principal, I possessed a Master's Degree in Educational Administration. However, as pastor I became part of the pastoral team for Calvary Community Church, which housed the school. This meant that I was also a member of the Elder Board of the Church, in addition to being on the School Board for the school. This made a busy schedule for me.

However, being the principal at M.C.S. was a very good experience for me. We rented a duplex for a while and then decided to buy our own home – the first home we had owned since Calgary about twenty years previously. It was very nice, and we were quite comfortable.

I was at Millwoods Christian School for six years as principal. During that time there were many challenges but also many good times. We had some problems related to losing staff and attendance of students in the school. This became a focus for me soon after I became principal. Our enrollment really had stagnated and wasn't going anywhere. I thought it was very ironic that we took several new teachers onto our staff (we focused on new teachers because of finances) and then when they became outstanding teachers we lost them mostly to Edmonton Public because of the higher salaries they could receive.

During my third year as principal, a board member who had the same vision I had decided with me to explore the options concerning Alternate status with Edmonton Public. We knew that Strathcona Christian Academy had successfully done so with their jurisdiction, and we felt that this would open many doors for our school. I discussed this with the school board on several occasions and for many hours because this was a dramatic turn from the reasons why the school had become a private school in the beginning.

After much discussion our school board and elder board both became united, stating that it would be a good thing for us to do as long as we could keep our principles and the faith in Christ that we had. A committee was established to negotiate with Edmonton Public officials. After several months of negotiation an agreement was finally reached and we were accepted into Edmonton Public as an Alternate School. This occurred during my fifth year as principal.

I was told that the learning curve would be very steep for me as far as becoming a principal in Edmonton Public and that was very true.

The Next Role That God Had For Me

When the steering committee from Prairie Junior/Senior High School learned of my experience in taking Millwoods Christian into alternate status they hired me as Principal with the purpose of working together with Golden Hills to help Prairie do the same. This was a year with many preparations taking place in anticipation of the change. This goal was successfully achieved within the year. It turned out that because of the disease, one year would be all that I would be there.

By the end of the school year, my speech had continued to deteriorate so that it had become difficult for me to speak at the graduation exercises, though this was my responsibility. With the prospects of having to teach classes under the auspices of Golden Hills, I knew that this would be impossible for me. The way things worked out was in God's plan, for I knew I had to quit because of this affliction.

How We Have Approached Trials in our Lives

Both my wife Ann and I thought that it would be important to demonstrate to you how God prepared us to go through trials, including the disease that I now have. We have seen many trials over the years, but God has used those to prepare us for this one, one of the greatest.

God has been very good to us throughout our lives, but we should also demonstrate how He has been with us through the hard times that we have faced. Our Lord has been faithful to us in using those trials to help us to grow. We have found at times that the road of life has been very bumpy with many turns and twists in it. There have been wonderful times of success but there have also been times of deep disappointment.

You will sometimes wonder how you will ever make it up the next hill because life's challenges are so steep. However, we have found that no matter what life's curves are before us, we can always depend on Jesus to be there beside us. He is always there to encourage us to persevere and never feel totally defeated. The following verse of scripture has been important to us: "*So do not fear, for I am with you; do not be dismayed, for I am your God. I will strengthen you and help you; I will uphold you with my righteous right hand.*" (Isaiah 41:10) God has shown us that we can have victory over the most difficult situations that we face.

There is another verse of scripture that we have found to be important when we are facing a trial. "*Be strong and courageous. Do not be afraid or terrified because of them, for the LORD your God goes with you; He will never leave you nor forsake you.*" (Deuteronomy 31:6) We have found this to be true. When we fall down He picks us up. When we get discouraged He sees our tears. He walks before us and we never have to walk alone. We have found Him to be our Guide and our Protector. When we are going through the roughest of times He will carry us through.

It has been exciting to know that God cares so much for us that He even knows the number of hairs on our head. Look how He takes care of the birds of the air! Are you not more important than these? Each day we face, we know that God knows what is before us and He will never allow anything more than what we can bear. We know that God is in control. Therefore no matter what happens we are safe in the arms of God.

Life's joys and struggles have helped us to grow in Christ He has helped us to put our roots deep into the ground so that we can stand strong against the storms of life. We know from experiences we have had that no matter what comes our way we can face it in that day. God is always there to strengthen us and to give us the guidance that we need. We encourage you to obtain that same confidence in God, so that you will know His power in your life each day.

Two Occupations Finished, a Third One Begins

Probably one of the biggest concerns with the illness affecting my speech was the fact that as a pastor I needed to speak a great deal. Also as a school administrator/teacher, speech is of paramount importance. Both occupations are now taken away from me. I knew that now I would have to remain at home and my wife would have to work. Thankfully, three days after we moved back to Edmonton, Ann returned to her old job. God is always there to help with every situation. We were also able to buy a new home, which we thank God for.

There is another occupation that I can become involved with, and that is to write books. For many years I had planned to write a book. Now, with this affliction it means that I have to write at least two books, because I also needed to write this book to help others who are in similar conditions. It could be that God can use me in this area as well.

In writing this chapter, I have made several references to God leading us in the life that we have lived. He has been faithful through every aspect of our lives - the bad times as well as the good. In the next chapter I want to focus more directly upon how God helps us and gives us hope in every situation.

Chapter Three:

How God Has Been My Help

I have talked of how God has been my help throughout my life as my Guide and Leader. In this chapter I want to focus on how God has helped me with this disease that has been placed upon me. God has truly been very faithful to me as I have had to walk through this valley. He has always been there for me – so close in fact that I don't really have too many concerns even though my life is in very real jeopardy. In future chapters I will amplify why God has given me a good attitude about the illness. First of all, I would like to explain what it means to accept Christ as your Saviour from a biblical perspective, and why it changed my life so totally.

Finding Jesus Christ as My Saviour

As I mentioned in the last chapter, when I was sixteen years old I found Christ as my Saviour. This did not happen the first time I attended a Youth Group meeting, nor did it happen the first time I attended church. It happened after I had been going for quite a long time. I accepted Christ after I had learned that I was born a sinner and that I needed to repent of those sins and invite Jesus to come into my life as I turned my life over to Him.

You see it takes time for an individual to consider where they stand in God's sight. You will never get that information from someone who does not know Jesus Christ as Saviour. No religion can teach this to you, and no tradition can teach you what you need to do. Where can you get the information? The only place is from the Bible, which is also known as the Word of God.

There are many who do not accept the fact that the Bible is God's truth. The reason for this attitude is that most do not want to acknowledge their own sin. They want to live any way that they please, and do not want to surrender to God. It is true that you can reject Christ as your Saviour. In fact most people do this. For some, however, when tragedy strikes, they become more willing to accept the fact that they do not have all of life's answers – only God has.

I pray that everyone who reads this book will understand that the Bible is true, and that it is the only book that can give the answers to life's toughest questions. Let me give you some verses of scripture that back up what I am saying about the fact that everyone lives in sin until they accept Christ. In Romans 3:23 we read: *"for all have sinned and fall short of the glory of God."* Here are some other verses that say the same thing:

> *The LORD saw how great man's wickedness on the earth had become, and that every inclination of the thoughts of his heart was only evil all the time* (Genesis 6:5).

> *Everyone has turned away, they have together become corrupt; there is no one who does good, not even one* (Psalm 53:3).

> *Who can say, "I have kept my heart pure; I am clean and without sin"?* (Proverbs 20:9)

> *We all, like sheep, have gone astray, each of us has turned to his own way; and the LORD has laid on Him the iniquity of us all.* (Isaiah 53:6)

> *All of us have become like one who is unclean, and all our righteous acts are like filthy rags; we all shrivel up like a leaf, and like the wind our sins sweep us away.* (Isaiah 64:6)

> *If we claim to be without sin, we deceive ourselves and the truth is not in us.* (1 John 1:8)

Please notice that the evidence from God's Word is very strong. Everyone who has ever lived was born in sin because of the sin of Adam, the first man on this earth. His sin passed on to everyone else who has ever lived. *"Therefore, just as sin entered the world through one man, and death through sin, and in this way death came to all men, because all sinned."* (Romans 5:12) This shows that because sin was brought into the world, all who are born must also die. Death is in the world and therefore sin is also.

In the Old Testament, the Jews lived under the Law. They covered their sins by animal sacrifices. The blood of bulls and goats covered their sin, but such an offering had to be made every time someone sinned. In the New Testament, Jesus came to die on a cross, thereby taking our sins upon Himself. The prophet Isaiah mentioned that above in Isaiah 53:6. If we come to the place that we realize our own sin, then God has the remedy for us. *"But God demonstrates his own love for us in this: while we were still sinners, Christ died for us,"* (Romans 5:8). We also read in John 3:16: *"For God so loved the world that He gave His one and only Son, that whoever believes in Him shall not perish but have eternal life."*

The biggest challenge is for us to believe that Jesus died for our sins. We need to put our faith in Him in order to be saved. We read what our obligations are to find eternal life: "*That if you confess with your mouth, 'Jesus is Lord,' and believe in your heart that God raised Him from the dead, you will be saved. For it is with your heart that you believe and are justified, and it is with your mouth that you confess and are saved.*" (Romans 10:9, 10)

If you are reading this book and you want to repent of your sins by asking Jesus into your life, then be assured that He will come and make his home with you. Your past ambitions will change, and suddenly you will have a different motivation in your life. I would really encourage you to start attending a Bible-believing church on a regular basis. You will need to read the Word of God daily. I suggest that you start in the New Testament, probably with the Gospel of John. That will demonstrate that Jesus Christ is God!

Please understand that Hell is a very real place. John 3:16 talked about not "perishing." What is meant there is that if you don't accept Christ as Saviour, you won't be accepted into Heaven when you die. Instead your soul will go to a place of torment, known as Hell. If you read the Bible (particularly the New Testament) you will find many references to Hell. In fact, there are more references to Hell than there are to Heaven. Here is one verse for you: "*Do not be afraid of those who kill the body but cannot kill the soul. Rather, be afraid of the One who can destroy both soul and body in hell.*" (Matthew 10:38) The One who can destroy both soul and body in Hell is God Himself.

Finding Christ as your Saviour is the most important step you can take in your life. This is the greatest step I ever took, because now with this illness I know that I am in good hands, whether I live or die! I would hope that you can say the same thing today.

The Importance of Christ Throughout My Life

As I mentioned in the last chapter, Christ was very central in everything we did. We have always done what we felt was God's will for us, regardless of the income that we would be getting, and regardless of the security in the job. A good example of this was when we left Rosebrier School to go to Calgary and start up a school. We were very secure in that school where I was the principal, and the pay as a teacher had been improving steadily. In fact, if I had chosen to remain as a school teacher and administrator, I would have been quite well off and by the time I reached the age of fifty-five I could have retired and lived fairly comfortably. I wouldn't have to be depending upon the Lord now for our income. Knowing this, we still felt following the Lord's will was paramount for our lives.

It is interesting that there were some people who thought I was very foolish to go into the ministry when we were planning to leave Calgary. The income, we knew, would be far less than what I had been getting. I knew that I would have to supplement my income by teaching on the side. Again, regardless of what men thought, we felt compelled to follow God's will. This has been the case throughout our lives.

Relating to my present condition, there was a time when I have really felt the healing touch of God in my life. During my thirties I had a chronic back problem that included the sciatic nerve in my right hip. After a long car ride I could not walk at times. Also there were several occasions when I had to sleep on the floor because of the pain in my back. I wore out two corsets, which had steel stays in them, trying to manage the pain.

I had been prayed for on numerous occasions but had not been healed. However, this time I decided that I had enough of the problem. At a Camp Meeting I felt God's healing presence and that I had to announce this to the people at the conclusion of the service (this all happened in the prayer time after the service was over). I announced that God had told me that I was going to be healed. I accepted that, and wore the corset no more. It took about six months before all the pain left, and I have never been bothered by sciatic pain since. In some ways I have the feeling that I need to do something similar today, but I don't know what.

Christ has always been with us, and I have always honoured Him by reading His Word on a daily basis as well as spending time in prayer. I feel His presence every day; in fact if I did not feel His presence I would become very concerned. I have dedicated my life to Him, and He can do whatever He wants with it. I am in His care, and I trust Him with my life and to watch over my family.

We have had many mountain top experiences in our lives, where we have felt God's blessing upon us in a wonderful way. However, we have also had several valley experiences as we mentioned earlier. We have seen our parents on both Ann's and my side all die. We have had many financial difficulties, but we also have seen God's blessings upon us in remarkable ways. For example, when we had just moved to the home near Thorsby, we had very little money but we had a crew working on our house.

In a country setting and you were expected to provide meals for any workers who came to your place. Ann was thinking that it would be nice to serve them ham for dinner. She went into the small town and looked at the prices but the hams were small and very expensive. Ann decided to come home and find something else to give them. In the meantime an older gentlemen named Alex was in Leduc. He had no way to know the desire of Ann's heart. He picked up a large ham plus numerous other groceries and delivered them to the door in time for Ann to make up the dinner for the crew. This was a sign to us that God cares about even the smallest details of our lives. God revealed Himself to us in many different ways and we can say to all that God is truly good.

Christ has been very important to me throughout my life, and He has constantly showed His care for me. That is why I can approach Him with confidence at any moment of the day. I know that He is watching over me and that He loves me a great deal (as He loves everyone on this planet!). Our God is a wonderful God!

How God Has Been Helping In My Present Condition

The changes in my mouth and throat have been outstanding. In about one year's time, I cannot talk or eat food. I sometimes feel less than human. As I watch television I see so many people happily eating food. They are having a very good time. I cannot have that kind of pleasure any more. We used to go out to restaurants occasionally, and we liked to go to dinner theatres from time to time. All that has now been taken away from me, and one would be prone to wonder where God is in all of this.

My tongue feels very weird at times, with small bits of things on it or with a hair going across the front of it. I have put my finger over my tongue to get such things out, only to find there is nothing there. The small bits, however, are real, and I understand that they come from my stomach. The A.L.S. Manual speaks of this: "Others may find that a hard toothbrush can be very helpful for removing build-up which occurs on the teeth, particularly after tube-feeding."[5]

---

[5] "Living With ALS," page 57

I have to pull my cheeks out at times during the night so that they won't get between my teeth. Sometimes I awaken at night with my cheek between my teeth. My appearance has changed quite a bit, though people say that I look really good for someone with my condition. My mouth looks like I am wearing a constant frown because the muscles that hold things in place have grown weak.

With these conditions, can it be said that God is still with me, and that He is blessing me? I say a resounding "Yes" to that! He is with me every step of the way. He gives me strength from day to day, and continually affirms His love for me. I would say though that it is critical for me to be reading the Bible regularly (I read about ten chapters a day). Without that, I would not have the strength that I now have. My times of prayer have also been precious because I know that He hears and answers prayer.

God has helped me to get feeling better after being in the hospital, getting pneumonia two months in a row. I was quite depressed about that, actually. I knew that my ordeal in January was worse than what I faced in December. I asked the Lord to keep pneumonia away from me for a long time because I was concerned that such an affliction could take my life. Therefore, I am very happy that I have gone through a few months without getting pneumonia! My lungs have been totally clear for about twenty days at the time I am writing this. If I can keep pneumonia away from me, I will be celebrating a great victory. God has been answering prayer on my behalf. I should also say that in June I got a nebulizer from the respiratory therapist who visits me each week. This is designed to keep me free from lung infections. I thank God for that!

Also, I asked God to strengthen my body, for I found myself to be very weak when I came out of the hospital. The pneumonia had taken a great deal out of me. I had gone through some surgery (for the first time) to get a PEG installed in my stomach, and I hadn't eaten anything for five days before the PEG was installed. I was also coughing somewhat after I came out of the hospital, and I was wondering if this was going to be a continuous thing for me because my lungs were clear when I left the hospital. When a respiratory therapist came to visit me, she did find some congestion in one of the lobes of my lungs. I was still on medication so that was cleared up quickly and now it has remained clear.

However I was still coughing even without an infection. I realized that it was my saliva that was doing this. I had two different anti-saliva medications and my local doctor suggested that I take both of them in amounts that would work for me. After I started taking them in combination, I was then controlling my saliva well and my coughing stopped. I now cough very little. I thank the Lord for directing me in this way, because now I am gaining strength back. I have now started taking a walk every day that is about thirty minutes long, walking quite quickly. My lungs are getting stronger, and I am feeling better all around.

I have found that I cannot sit around and feel sorry for myself. That won't do me any good. That is why writing is a good therapy for me. I know that I cannot do things that everyone else can do, but that is okay. I am still alive, and I can minister to others even now. When people come to visit, I need to use my voice synthesizer to talk to them. This can be awkward at times, but God has used me to be a blessing to others. I thank Him for that!

Will God heal me from this malady? Much of this discussion I want to reserve for my next chapter, but let it be known that I have talked to God a great deal about that. I haven't yet received and answer from Him, but I have felt His loving presence in a remarkable way at times. I have told people this fact: I will be blessed no matter what happens in the future. I will receive a tremendous blessing if God restores my health to me, but I will receive an even greater blessing if He takes me home to be with Him! You see, I am blessed either way! Taking me home wouldn't be a blessing for my family though (not at this time, anyway. If I one day need twenty-four hour supervision, that concept might change.)

Taking me away from my ability to work in my professions has been a concern for me. However, God has replaced that with something that hopefully will be a blessing for others. He always is there to watch over me and to demonstrate His care for me. I was getting old enough to retire from that kind of life anyway. As I told my daughter and son-in-law last fall, I am kind of happy to be out of that rat race. I have handled a lot of difficulties as an administrator, so I don't need that any more. They both are administrators as well as teachers in Millwoods Christian School, which is growing very quickly now because it has become an Alternate School within Edmonton Public.

I simply am giving myself totally over to God. He can do whatever He wants. "*And we know that in all things God works for the good of those who love Him, who have been called according to His purpose,*" (Romans

8:28). I thank God that I can stand upon His Word, and I know that He is in control of my situation!

There is something else that I have done in order to have His Word in front of me at all times. I found several verses from the Bible that have to do with healing and God's faithfulness. I prepared them on PowerPoint and converted them to "jpeg". Through a program I have downloaded, they change on my desktop every few seconds. I also have them as my screensaver so that I see the Word constantly if I am not using a program.

That didn't seem to be enough for me, however. More recently I have found more verses that deal with healing and the need I have for God's help. They fill up nine pages. I read them over and meditate on them as much as I can each week, asking the Lord to honour His Word in my life. Who knows, this might bring about my healing one day. If it doesn't, it surely gets me into the Word anyway!

God has been helping me a great deal. I really don't know how I could manage if He wasn't with me all of the time. The Holy Spirit is truly my Comforter these days. To me, this is all that I need. I will do what I can with the days that I have left. I have asked Him for enough time to finish both of the books that I have started. If He gives me longer, I will write more! I believe that He can minister to people through what I write.

How God Helped Me to Have a Proper Focus on Faith

I realize that even for a Christian in this situation it is sometimes difficult to have faith when your world seems to be crashing down all around you. There were times when I admit that I did not have the kind of faith I needed. I still have a lot of questions for God, as I will talk about in the next chapter.

Actually I never did lose faith in God. I have always believed that God is with me and that He has the power to heal me. It could be said that I was at a place where I was accepting death as God's will for me. In fact that might still be the case, but I have come to realize that I must exercise faith at all times. By faith, great things can be accomplished, but without faith nothing can be done. We read: *"And without faith it is impossible to please God, because anyone who comes to Him must believe that He exists and that He rewards those who earnestly seek Him."* (Hebrews 11:6) This shows us that God wants us to have faith. Without demonstrating a real, living faith, we cannot please Him. In some ways I think I was lacking in the kind of faith that would bring about my healing. I do thank God for showing me that I needed to approach Him in faith, believing that He will heal me.

Through God's help, I came to realize that I must exercise faith in His healing power at all times, and claim my healing. Therefore, I now regularly pray for healing, and as I said, I read those verses through a few times each week. God is always there, to keep me encouraged and full of hope. I know I can rest in Him because He will work all things out for my good (Romans 8:28). He is all-powerful (omnipotent) and it would be a very small thing for Him to heal my body. Perhaps I have to do my part and believe that a miracle will come my way soon. I am claiming that each day!

In some ways I believe that I am in a spiritual war, as several people have stated. Satan wants to destroy me, so what he did to Job he is doing to me, feeling that I won't have the faith to claim my healing. He also wants to discourage me on a daily basis. Therefore it is important that I strengthen myself even as Jude wrote: *"But you, dear friends, build yourselves up in your most holy faith and pray in the Holy Spirit. Keep yourselves in God's love as you wait for the mercy of our Lord Jesus Christ to bring you to eternal life."* (Jude 20, 21) With God's help, I intend to build myself up on a regular basis, knowing that without God's power in my life, I cannot do anything. It is my desire to access the throne room of God on a regular basis until the power of Satan is broken. Hopefully at that point I can realize a complete healing for my body.

How do I know if God still wants me around? Maybe He wants to take me home after all. However, if He is the One who is trying my faith to purify me, then I will work to increase my faith. I will discuss the need for faith in a future chapter of this book.

Other Ways God Has Helped Me

My whole focus on life has changed quite a bit. For example, I have a great deal of love for food and I loved to eat. It has been difficult for me to smell good food and not to be able to partake of it. However, the nutrition program that I am on probably gives me a better diet than I had before. I always wanted to lose weight but did not succeed in doing that. Now, however, my stomach gets very full with the tube feeding that I have. Therefore, I really don't long to have regular food, even though I sometimes dream about it. I have now lost over thirty pounds, so my body looks better than it did before. A lot of my fat is gone. That is good, but the way it happened cannot be considered the best way. I do keep my body weight very uniform. At the present time my weight is pretty static.

I have also realized more than ever before that natural food is not really the most important for me. Rather, it is spiritual food that is most important. While regular food has been taken away, my spiritual food is much better than it has been before. My focus has been turned to the spiritual much more than to the physical. I have some severe limitations in talking to people but there are no limitations to me talking to God. He is willing to listen to anything I have to say, and His blessing is always there to comfort me.

I have also been visited by family members as well as by friends much more than I ever had before. People are driving several miles to come to see me, and I am very thankful for that. It is good to see friends again. It is especially good when they come individually or as couples because I can communicate with them better with my voice synthesizer.

Daily I need to be thankful to God, because each day He gives me the strength that I need. Each day He is there for me, to help me in every situation. I am sure that if He desires to take me home, my blessing will be greater there than I can even imagine. However, I also know that as long as I am here, He will also use me to be a blessing to others. I want Him to use me as long as I have the ability to do so. I am very thankful that I still have use of my arms and legs, and I still can breathe quite normally. Praise God for His care over me! I encourage you to seek the Lord today so that He can be as great a blessing to you as He is to me.

God Has Given to Me a Strong Support System

I realize that some who read this book might nor have the strong support system that I have. To fight such an illness you need to have a strong support system, and I hope that you will be able to access such a system. God has been very good to me in this regard. There are basically two groups that have given me strong support.

My Family

I have talked some about my wife Ann, who has been a tremendous support for me on a daily basis. Actually she is the one who needs more help than I do as far as her being able to cope with the illness. However, she has always been there for me through everything. When I was in the hospital she was faithful to visit me for a long time each day even though she was working full time. She also arranges to take time off (she has a very flexible schedule) to come with me to every appointment I have. She is my voice as well with all of the doctors and therapists who I see, because they cannot always understand what I say.

I haven't written very much about my four children who are now adults (three of them are married with families). We have always been a very close family and for a while we lived in the same area of the city. We are very close in distance for three of our children now. Trevor and his family have recently answered the call from God to move to New Zealand to begin a ministry there. However, Trevor is probably more in touch with us now than he was when they lived very close to us. Trevor has since moved back home to be with us.

Jacqueline married Dan, and they both are teachers and administrators at Millwoods Christian School. Jacqueline has made the Home School program very successful at the school, and Dan is being an outstanding leader in the High School, helping students to achieve their very best. He has had wonderful results. Dan has been a tremendously supportive son-in-law for us.

Trevor and Shawn both became pastors. It was something that we never encouraged because of the hardships that are connected with ministry. They have both developed into very good speakers and we are especially happy that they have followed God's calling in their lives. This is very important to us.

Trevor had pastored in Edmonton for several years before they felt God's call to New Zealand. While Trevor was pastoring, his wife Karen was involved in some pretty high forms of research, involving the nervous system. It is interesting that this disease now affects my nervous system! Karen was also involved in writing a research document for the medical field. In moving home, she has returned to the same lab.

Both Trevor and Karen are allowing God to move them into a wider dimension for their ministries. Karen has really blossomed spiritually as well! We are very happy for them. God is using them and leading them into new vistas that are needed in this world today.

Shawn is Associate Pastor in the church that his father-in-law is senior pastor. In their case PK's (pastors' kids) married each other. Shawn has developed into an administrator as well as developing a real ministry with regards to spiritual warfare. Shawn's wife Shirley is an Occupational Therapist by trade, and she has been a tremendous help to me with regards to me adapting to the changes the illness has brought.

Janine is the only child of ours who is not yet married at the time of this writing. She is working on her own, with the idea of developing a ministry with regards to sports. She has a very good network of friends who are assisting her. Janine and her friends are contacting people all over the world to pray for me, and we have received several reports of how people on every continent have been praying. In this way, she has been a great support to me.

Together, our family has been very supportive, visiting us, praying for us, and helping in any way that they can. They have been a tremendous blessing to us throughout their lives, and we are very thankful to God for them. They also have a strong faith that God is going to heal me.

The Professional Health Supporters

I have mentioned some of these people previously, but I do want to give thanks to God for each one of them. I realize that in some areas this kind of care is not available and so I know that God has blessed me greatly. I think of the doctors who have been involved.

When I was hospitalized I met the head of the Neurological Department who was a great encouragement to me. My own doctor, Dr. Siddiqi, has been of great assistance when I have been sick and otherwise. Doctors that I met during the night in the Emergency Department, whose names I do not even remember, still were very prominent in helping me to feel better. Dr. Kalra and Dr. Siddiqi are both associated with the A.L.S. clinics that I attend on a monthly basis (sometimes more than monthly). They are very helpful in teaching me how to look after myself.

My own personal physician, Dr. Myrholm, has been of invaluable assistance. He even came to my home to check me out the last time I had pneumonia. It was through his advice that I went to the Emergency

Department to get accepted into the hospital. He also sees to it that I get the medications that I need.

At home, I have been helped by respiratory nurses and a nurse practitioner who will come to see me if and when I start coughing again. They are experts in this area, and understand my situation very well. The Home Care nurse came and helped Ann to set up a system for me to take a tremendous amount of different medications the last time I came home from the hospital. She supplied us with various sizes of syringes for me to use for my medications (all medications are taken through the feeding tube, so they are in liquid form). The Nutrition Program involves a speech pathologist, a nurse, and an occupational therapist, all of whom have been very helpful. I thank God for each one of them, who have been used by God to help me in my situation.

It was also through the Health Nurse that we were able to obtain a suction machine that I use frequently when I cough, or when I am having difficulties with saliva. The A.L.S. Society and the ICAN Center at the Glenrose Hospital provided us with a voice synthesizer free of charge, and I thank God for that. Without that my ability to say something would be extremely limited. Through the A.L.S. Society I was also able to obtain a special bed with no cost to us. It is an electronic bed that rises at its head or foot by remote control. I always need to sleep with my head raised each night so that my breathing is not impaired and so my food stays in my stomach.

Truly, God has been very good to me with regards to the support system that I have. My family is of tremendous help to me, as have been the professional people. God has been good to me through this all, and I praise Him for that

Chapter Four:

Questions I Have Had For God

There are a lot of questions that I have been asking God about. This doesn't mean that I am lacking in faith but it does show some definite concerns that I have with respect to me getting this disease. I suppose everyone who is going through similar circumstances that I am probably have the same kind of questions when facing death. The problem is that there are no real answers to many of these questions.

However, I expect to get answers to these when I die and go to heaven. If God heals me, then I will probably forget the questions that I have now. In the meantime, my condition is not improving. Last week I was feeling pretty good, but for the last four days I have been coughing more because of excess saliva which now seems to be coming back. I thought I had it under control very well, but for some reason the medication is not working the way it was at first.

I am writing this book as the disease is progressing. Therefore, even though I wrote of the progression of the disease in the first chapter, I will update you as I write more chapters, especially when something important is revealed. I will start with an update before getting into the main part of this chapter.

An Update of My Condition

Yesterday (March 8th) I went to an A.L.S. clinic and there we were talking to Dr. Kalra, the specialist in charge. He was concerned about the amount of saliva I had and prescribed more of one drug that I had for handling the saliva. I have to still adjust what is the best amount to take of the other medication for it.

Before we went to the clinic, I had to get a pulmonary test done first. The results of that were not good. My breathing was poorer than it had been before; with the biggest problem being that I was not able to exhale very well after I had inhaled. This meant that carbon dioxide was probably staying in my lungs, making me tired during the day.

I may have to get what is called a "biPap" which will involve a mask that I will have to wear at night. This is supposed to make my breathing more normal. I will spend a couple of days in an Intensive Care Unit at the Misercordia Hospital in order to get set up with the machine. I expect that it will take some time to get used to using it.

The biggest news, however, is that my pulmonary test indicates that the disease is moving downwards into my lungs. I found out from the doctor how most people die when the disease affects lungs. Usually people get more and more tired because of the lack of oxygen. Eventually death comes while the patient is sleeping, because he or she doesn't wake up any more. To me this is not a bad way to die – in fact it is a pretty good way. I was a bit disturbed though, to see how fast the disease is progressing. My time seems to be coming to an end pretty soon. However, I feel I need some time to get this book done as well as some other things.

Now I will get on with the main part of this chapter, relating to questions that I have for God.

Why Did This Happen To Me?

This disease, though it is not classified as a rare disease, is not heard of too often. I certainly had not been very familiar with it. Therefore I have to wonder, why I was given this disease that robs me of my roles as pastor or principal/teacher. This was a difficult question for me to deal with, because it changed my life quickly. All of a sudden I could not do either profession.

The answer was, I believe, that God wanted to lead me into a new area of ministry – that involved writing books, though with the sudden progression of this disease means that I might not be able to write very many. I would suggest though, that my writing might reach more people than my pastoring or my work as an administrator. I hope that is true, and that my words can influence a lot of people.

Concerning the terminal form of the disease, there is of course no cure for this affliction. It automatically ends in death, though many people have lived for several years with ALS. I happened to get the most rapid form of it, and it is progressing even more quickly in me than the same form has progressed in other people. In many ways I have no complaints about that, because I'd rather go to be with the Lord than to suffer. But it does make me wonder why I, who have served God for almost my entire life, should be afflicted with such a disease.

Who Gave This Disease to Me, God or Satan?

This is a huge question that has theological implications. We know that God has put diseases upon people in the past, but weren't those wicked people that He did this to? The greatest example was the plagues that God brought upon the Egyptians.

> He said, "If you listen carefully to the voice of the LORD your God and do what is right in His eyes, if you pay attention to His commands and keep all His decrees, I will not bring on you any of the diseases I brought on the Egyptians, for I am the LORD, Who heals you." (Exodus 15:26)

We know, of course that, the Israelites did sin greatly. Because of their sin, they eventually were afflicted with all sorts of diseases. We see that God Himself is the One who promises healing to His people. One of the names for God is actually found from the above verse. *"Jehovah-Rophe"* means, "The Lord, our Healer." This is one of my collections of verses on healing.

There are several verses in which God promises to afflict His people with diseases if they are unfaithful to Him. But He also promises to heal:

> The moon will shine like the sun, and the sunlight will be seven times brighter, like the light of seven full days, when the LORD binds up the bruises of His people and heals the wounds He inflicted (Isaiah 30:26).

Here we see that God had inflicted wounds upon His people. However He had done so because they had sinned and were far away from Him. Eventually, He caused both of Northern and the Southern Kingdoms of Israel to be conquered by enemy forces and exiled to far away lands. God does not wink at sin, but He rather judges His own people if they are in sin. We cannot escape His punishment if we are living far away from Him.

How does this refer to me? Well, I don't think that I have lived in a wicked fashion so that God has wanted to punish me. That then brings me to Satan, otherwise known as the devil. I believe that Satan has put this upon me, even as he put the affliction upon Job. The book of Job asks the question, "Why do the righteous suffer?" We see the discussion between God and Satan in Chapters One and Two of the book of Job.

This person was set up by God as a righteous person who lived a good life, so Satan was given the opportunity to afflict pain upon him in order to get Job to turn his back on God. Satan however, was not allowed to kill Job. He was not given a terminal disease, though everything was taken away from him.

I have recently been reading the Book of Job. It is quite interesting to read this book after I have been afflicted with the disease that I have. One verse really popped out at me because I was seeing how Job felt with the affliction that he had. I have some similar feelings as Job had: *"According to Your knowledge I am indeed not guilty, yet there is no deliverance from Your hand."* (Job 10:7 NASB) This indeed is an interesting verse in that I am looking for God to heal me, but so far He has not done that. Job also had that question in His mind. By the way, I probably have been suffering with this longer than Job had to with his affliction!

One day after prayer I felt that Satan had put this upon me. Therefore I wrote up a document that I gave to my family members. I quote some of that here, indicating that I feel that Satan has put this upon me because of previous accidents that I had. These caused some whiplashes to my neck, the area which has been affected. God has permitted him to do this, knowing that I will not turn my back on Him but actually draw closer to Him. Here is a paragraph from what I wrote in that document:

> To be honest, I had felt that if the Lord wanted to take me home that was okay as far as I was concerned. However, I have come to the conclusion that I do not want to die because of something that Satan has put upon me. I am willing to die if I have finished my course and God was ready to take me home. At fifty-eight years old, I think that there is a great deal more I can do for God, particularly in the area of preparing the Church for Christ's return.[6]

With the idea that Satan has put this upon me, it means that to be healed, Satan's power in this area must be broken. This is where real spiritual warfare must come in. Since I am in my condition, I confess that I am not really powerful in this area. Therefore I need Christians who are willing to become prayer warriors to intercede on my behalf. I know that this is happening already, by some people that I don't even know. I have heard the comments from several and for many months that this is a spiritual warfare, and Satan must be defeated. He was actually defeated when Christ died for us on the Cross and was resurrected, but he needs to be defeated concerning the affliction he put upon me.

---

[6] "Why God Allowed Satan to Put This Affliction Upon Me"

I am in the place where I need God's healing touch very soon. There is another verse of scripture that means a lot to me in this regard: *"Then your light will break forth like the dawn, and your healing will quickly appear; then your righteousness will go before you, and the glory of the LORD will be your rear guard."* (Isaiah 58:8) I am trusting in God to heal me quickly! Satan's power is already broken because of the Cross. As a church we need to take authority over him!

Will God Heal Me?

This is another big question that I have been asking God for quite a while. As I mentioned earlier, this is something for which I must exercise faith. I am believing that God will heal me. However, faith can be a struggle sometimes, especially when you don't see the answer coming. I will look at this more in Chapter Six.

I feel that I could do a great deal more for Him in this world if He chooses to heal me. I am at such a place in this illness that it would be a great miracle. This disease has really done a number on me. Neurons that have been deadened would have to spring to life again. Muscles in my neck and mouth that have atrophied would have to be given new strength and new life. All of this would be a tremendous miracle, and I would surely be ready to tell many others of the work that God has done in my body.

There certainly has been a great deal of prayer for me. With today's technology, people from all over the world have heard of the affliction and are praying for me. I know that churches in the United States are praying for me, as well as a church in Nigeria. Several individual people have prayed for me from Japan to the United States and to points beyond. I know of people who have been awakened at night to intercede for me. In Prairie Bible Institute at Three Hills there are people praying for me on a regular basis. Truly there have been many people praying for me, but no healing has come at this time.

There have also been prophecies pronounced over me (you may not believe in prophecies, but I certainly do, as long as they line up with scripture). Several prophecies have mentioned the fact that I would have to get to a pretty low state before healing would come. Well I am very quickly reaching that place, so I trust that healing will come soon! I will share those prophecies later in this book.

I really don't know if God is going to heal me, but I am believing that He will. That means that Satan's power has to be broken. There is another passage of scripture in this theme that God made very real to me today: *"You know what has happened throughout Judea, beginning in Galilee after the baptism that John preached– how God anointed Jesus of Nazareth with the Holy Spirit and power, and how He went around doing good and healing all who were under the power of the devil, because God was with Him."* (Acts 10:37, 38) Notice that here it seems those that were sick were under the power of the devil, the same as I am. But Jesus healed them all, and He can do the same for me. I am believing that He will do that.

Why Must I Suffer in Such a Way?

This is another important question that I have been asking God. If He is ready to take me home, there certainly would be other ways that I could die very quickly. I certainly will not have to suffer as long as many others do, but God could strike me dead in a second. Why should it take so long? This has been a very trying situation for my family, and especially for my wife who has seen the disease causing changes coming very quickly. It is hard for her not being able to understand what I am saying, and she sees how my body is becoming weaker as time passes.

For me there seems to be complications taking place on a regular basis. For example, I think I have my coughing under control, and then I suddenly begin coughing again, though my lungs are clear. Saliva is not being controlled, as it should be. That means the amount of my medication needs to be changed so that the saliva can be controlled.

There are other concerns that I have, some of which have been mentioned before. The biggest concern is getting pneumonia again and choking on phlegm. Dying that way is not something I want but the threat is always there.

Then there is the humiliation that I face from day to day. If I had pride in my heart, the Lord certainly has taken that away! I have manifestations such as coughing and spraying saliva over people in front of me. To prevent this I need to have a handkerchief in front of my face when I cough. Drooling also makes it appear to people like I have mental problems. When I brush my teeth, I have to bend over the sink so I don't get moisture over the front of my shirt. When I am coughing a lot, the front of my shirt gets wet with saliva. All of this is an extreme humiliation that I wish I didn't have to face. But all of these are part of the disease. In other areas, because my emotions are affected by this disease, I am very quick to cry and shed tears, sometimes making loud noises, when I see something that touches my heart. Again, this is a huge humiliation that I could do without.

Humiliation is caused by other facts as well. I have worked hard all my life, and been the major bread earner in our home. Now the two professions I was involved with are taken away from me. I basically have to stay at home now. I don't get out very often. For communicating to others I have to depend upon my wife to a great extent. All of this can be frustrating, especially if I dwell on it. My life has taken on a ninety-degree turn, and I sometimes feel that I'm on the outside looking in.

The question I ask God is "why me?" Why do I have to suffer such things, instead of dying with dignity? For some reason, this disease has come upon me, and with it humiliation. This is really a question that I don't have an answer for, but I hope to get that answer from God some day.

I suppose this is where faith and trust come in. Even though I cannot understand all of this, I do have to trust that God knows what is best, and He will work all things together for my good.

How Will My Wife Be Looked After?

We have chosen a lifestyle in which we always wanted to follow God's will for us regardless of the income that ministry would give to us. This we always did, believing that God would help us with the finances we needed. He always has done that. We haven't ever been prosperous, but we have generally lived comfortably. However, with me gone from the scene, I have been concerned about how Ann would fare in my absence as far as finances are concerned but also in the adjustments that she will have to make.

This is another question that I have asked God. I do know that God will take care of her in my absence, but losing me could be a big problem for her. She is learning to be quite independent, so if she really seeks the Lord, He will help to bring her out of the pain she might be facing. Strong help from our family also should help her in this situation. I am actually praying that God will bless her abundantly after I am gone. If I am healed of course, that would be a great blessing for her. However I am believing that if I am to be taken home by God that He will also bring a great blessing to her to help her in the years to come. Again, this is where trust in God comes from. If He has looked after us throughout our lives, I am sure that He will continue to look after Ann even if I am removed from the scene. I am praying for a bigger blessing that she has ever known would come to her to release all concerns that she might have.

Is There Something I Should Do In Order to Be Healed?

I ask this question as well because this often has gone through my mind. I have searched my own heart several times to see if there is some sin within my life. I receive temptations from the devil, of course, just like every other believer does. However, it is only when we yield to that temptation we commit sin. So far, I have kept my heart as pure as I think I can. There are always higher paths that the Lord wants us to climb to. Possibly that is what He has in His mind for me. I certainly struggle with effective prayer because of the hard times I have to stay awake. Somehow I have to either get enough sleep or learn how to draw closer to God in my situation.

I have tried not to become angry at anyone, and I have tried to demonstrate Jesus to others, even though my communication is not too good. I think that others consider me in the right light – that God does have His hand upon me. I do want to dwell very close to God.

Certainly I take time for God every day, and I pray every day, though I cannot say that I spend a lot of time in concerted prayer each day. As I said previously, I read ten chapters a day and meditate upon certain scripture verses. As I read a promise, I pause to ask God to fulfill His Word in my life. I usually have a very good time with God throughout the day, and feel His presence with me continually. When visitors come to visit me they almost always take time to pray for me.

There is something that we must be careful about, I feel. It is that we don't depend upon works in order for God to heal us. It is true that we have certain works to do to make sure our hearts are right in God's sight. However, works are not as important with regards to healing as simple faith is.

We must simply believe for salvation – it is not a matter of works. *"For it is by grace you have been saved, through faith–and this not from yourselves, it is the gift of God– not by works, so that no one can boast."* (Eph. 2:8, 9) We can never work our way into heaven. I believe that in the same way, God honours the faith that we have so we do not have to be concerned with trying to earn our healing. The subject of faith is a big one, especially when you have a terminal disease.

Can I Be Effective For God in My Present State?

As people read the books He gives me time to write, I know I will be as effective for God as possible. I believe this book will help many who are going through similar situations and it will help all believers who face ongoing trials. Most people do face trials regularly. It is part of life.

I think that I can be an encouragement to my family, though they find it difficult to see me in my condition sometimes. Ann would miss me a great deal if I were to die, as would the rest of my family. I simply have to use the experience that I have and the knowledge that I have to minister to individuals from time to time. It is when people visit us that I can be the most effective in ministering to them. Even my voice synthesizer can be important to me when I am able to help others in their situations. Therefore I can be effective to a limited extent in my present condition.

If I were healed, I could be much more effective. For example, I could go on book tours as most authors do in order to promote my books. I could speak in churches that have been praying for me, demonstrating that their prayers have been answered in a remarkable way. I also feel that I could develop a healing ministry.

If God healed me from this kind of a disease, certainly He could use me to see many others healed. In the section about our ministry in Thorsby, I mentioned that God had used us in this way before. We saw some dramatic healings take place at that time. So you can see that we are familiar with God using us to minister to others. This could be an avenue of ministry that would open to us.

We also have thought of going on short term missions' assignments in order to encourage missionaries who are working hard for God. We felt that we could be effective in this way in foreign fields where missionaries are labouring. We need to do what we can to win people to the Lord before it is too late. Obviously I need to be healed in order to do something like that.

Is My Usefulness on Earth Over in God's Eyes?

When considering the fact that a fatal disease with no cure has come upon me, I frequently have asked this question. In the previous question, I demonstrated that I think I could be effective for God, especially if He decided to heal me. However, there are areas in which I am getting too old for.

Pastoring a church, for example, would be hard to do at my age when younger couples need to be reached with the gospel. Also, I haven't taught school for many years, and that the door possibly would be shut for that - though I could probably substitute teach. Administrative positions would most likely be closed for me because jurisdictions usually encourage teachers they raise up to become administrators. If it were mine to choose, I would do the same. Therefore the professions that I have been doing throughout my lifetime would probably be closed to me anyway, even if God healed me.

I really don't know what God is considering with respect to my usefulness. My vision, of course, is quite limited compared to His. It might be His idea that I have outlived my usefulness on this earth, and that the time has come to take me home. Who can understand what God's will might be in this instance? His understanding is infinite, and He knows the future much better than any of us do. I certainly won't complain, if that is His desire!

God's ways are much higher than ours: *"As the heavens are higher than the earth, so are My ways higher than your ways and My thoughts than your thoughts."* (Isaiah 55:9) We can never attain to His thoughts and His ways while we are in these bodies. Of course, we must try to live in holiness because God is holy, but we cannot be compared to Him. We might try to emulate His love for us by loving others. I'm afraid that we would have to die in someone else's place to be able to copy His love more closely. God's ways are much higher, and much different from our ways. He is much superior to us in all of these areas.

Therefore I am not sure that I could be effective for God if I was healed. That is up to God to judge. As a result, I won't try to think I can understand His ways for my life. I simply have to rest in Him and believe that He will work all things out for my good.

Conclusion

Such are my questions that I have been asking God. I do feel that if you are going through a similar situation in your own life that you would have many of the same kind of questions for God. With our finite minds we cannot always understand God's ways of doing things. I simply have to rest in Him and trust Him in all things. That is about all I can do at this time. I certainly don't have all the answers but I know that God has them.

Chapter Five:

The Difficulties with Adjustments

In less than one year, I have had a tremendous amount of changes take place in my body. They are the kind I could not have ever comprehended. In this chapter I will relate some of them that have taken place quite suddenly. Changes are taking place quite regularly; in fact, its seems to be a period of constant, continuous change. The latest is written in the update that I gave to you in my last chapter. It is God Who has helped me to walk through these changes. Without Him they would be very difficult.

My Ability to Speak

This was probably my first dramatic change and one of the more difficult ones that occurred. I had the ability to speak very well. I preached twice each Sunday for fifteen years. Many who heard me would encourage me with comments about the good job I did. As a teacher and principal I was able to speak very clearly and distinctly.

When my speech began to deteriorate last April leading some to wonder if I had a stroke, it was a dramatic change to be faced with. I always shared devotions with my staff on Monday mornings but by June this was getting very hard to do and I had difficulties talking to the parents at the Graduation of our Grade Twelve students.

This was an enormous change for me. I knew that my days as teacher/administrator were coming to an end because I could no longer enunciate my words very clearly. I was bewildered. Even though there had been no official diagnosis at this time, I suspected it was probably bulbar ALS. The prospect that speaking could deteriorate further was the greatest shock.

Very quickly speech became a real problem for me. In the memoirs that I was keeping, early in August I wrote the following about my ability to speak:

> Speech is especially frustrating because what I say often isn't what I am thinking at times. I have to stop what I am saying sometimes and say it again for people to understand. It seems I

often have to repeat what I have said. I always need to have water handy to sip because my throat feels awkward, and water seems to soothe it. Also I get thirsty very quickly. My mind is as good as always, but my speech is a definite problem.[7]

While my family could understand me - and Ann was the best because she lived with me - others were having a harder time. When I was speaking on the phone, some people had a very hard time to understand. More than simply going through the suddenness of the change I also had to work a lot harder to try to say words in the right way. By September I noticed I had to repeat what I was saying more than before.

In the middle of August I had an appointment to see a speech pathologist to test what I was saying and rate its understandability. It was quite an extensive analysis. They recorded my speech and had others listen and critique it. At that time eighty percent of what I said could be understood.

However, the downward spiral continued very quickly. It wasn't many months before my own family could not understand what I said. My voice became the poorest when I came home from the hospital in January. Now my wife cannot understand what I am saying some of the time.

Now I have to use my voice synthesizer whenever I speak to others - even to Ann. The voice synthesizer is very effective when speaking one-to-one. It is more difficult to use when many people are present because with a lot of people talking it is hard to hear across the room. Getting used to using the voice synthesizer is one of my biggest adjustments.

To be honest, it has been disconcerting when people cannot understand me. I sometimes wonder 'what is the sense of saying anything?' It is very difficult for me to get involved in discussions, especially in a big crowd of people. I have a tendency to withdraw from speaking since people cannot understand.

However, at an A.L.S. clinic I attended a speech pathologist came to visit me. She gave me pointers that will help me to get adapted to the voice synthesizer. It takes time to learn how to effectively use it. I do

---

[7] "Thoughts Regarding a Fatal Disease," page 3

thank God for the technology that I have at my disposal. I just have to get proficient in its use.

Being in Hospital Quite Frequently With Pneumonia

As a pastor I frequently visited those who were ill but I have hardly ever been to a hospital as a patient. As a young boy I was admitted to the hospital with knee problems. As an adult I was in the hospital once with infectious hepatitis. I was very sick and was hospitalized for about one week. Outside of those times I was never in the hospital as a patient.

I was always quite healthy, so having to spend time in the hospital two months in a row was a big change. All of a sudden I understood the seriousness of my condition and I understood I could die by choking on phlegm. It was a great concern.

I had never been operated on before, and putting a PEG in my stomach was quite a first-time experience. I was semi-conscious during the surgery. They put an endoscope into my stomach to know exactly where to cut into my abdomen. It involved very little pain. I didn't feel anything until after the surgery was over. Being hospitalized was very new and being operated on was quite a change. But the biggest change came as a result of the PEG being installed.

No Longer Eating Food

Until early December I was eating regular food by just cutting everything in very small chunks and taking small bites of everything. It would take me about forty-five minutes to eat a meal. When I went to the hospital in December they felt I needed to have my food refined even more and so they put me on minced. We bought ourselves a food processor and were able to cut up all my food very finely. This was an adjustment, but I thought I was functioning quite well.

When we went to California for Christmas, I had difficulty eating food. I choked on a very small piece of chicken and required a Heimlich maneuver. Returning home, we continued to puree food - but I still ended up in the hospital with pneumonia. When I got out of the hospital I had to feed myself directly to my stomach. All this happened within a month and a half. This was a big change for me because food is something that I enjoy very much.

Before I had the PEG installed in the hospital, I hadn't eaten anything for five days. Doctors believed that I obtained the pneumonia through aspirating my own saliva - that means my own saliva went into my lungs. This necessitates I get rid of my saliva.

I pretty well have settled into the routine needed for medication and tube feedings. All the medication goes into my stomach by the tube. Following the medication, I give myself the food. The food has all the nutrients I need so I don't have to worry about my diet and my stomach usually gets quite full so I don't have to think about being hungry. But I agree with the professionals, it is good to have some snacks once in awhile just to be able to taste something good.

I lost a lot of weight while I was in the hospital but once I got on the tube feeding my weight remains just about the same every day. It usually varies about one-half a pound every day if there are any changes.

There are other issues related to food of which you may not be aware. I've noticed how many food commercials are on television. Things look really good and food smells delicious when we are at someone's place for dinner, or when Ann cooks up something herself.

I have been telling Ann not to worry about me as far as eating food is concerned. She needs to eat even though I can't. I am still in the adjustment stages vis-à-vis the smell and the look of food. I simply have to not be concerned about that. Having a full stomach most of the time helps and I am adjusting to not eating through my mouth.

Recently I have begun to cook meat for my wife and our daughter Janine on the barbeque. I had always done this before when I could eat regular foods, so I thought that I could be a blessing for them if I continued to do so. It actually hasn't been too hard for me to do this, indicating that I am adjusting.

In the beginning, the food I was taking by the gravity tube took over an hour to complete and I had to take it four times a day. However, since I have been on the feeding program, they gave me a larger tube so that I can finish eating in less then one half an hour and usually around twenty minutes. I only have to take it three times a day. Therefore the time is not too bad any more.

As you can see, it has been quite an adjustment to learn to have all my food through a tube instead of eating. I am gradually getting used to that. I also have to adapt to the fact that I take a lot more medication now than I did before. Before I only took one or two pills every day. Now I have about five different medications to take and more if I get an infection again. Because this can vary for time to time, I have to adapt to that quite often.

My food diet is quite different. It is all canned liquids. I don't taste it at all. The nutritionists say that it doesn't taste very good and I can believe it. It is for the stomach, not for the taste buds.

The waste that comes when the food is digested has a tendency of packing up, giving the person constipation. I was almost never constipated before I got the feeding tube, and now I have to take laxatives almost on a daily basis. This again is a big change for me - and not always a comfortable one. It is something that I simply have to learn to live with.

Otherwise the food is okay. And it is probably cheaper than if I regularly ate through the mouth - we enjoyed going to a restaurant once in awhile. While the food I take in is not very tasty, it does extend my life, so I am thankful for that.

The Need to Handle Saliva

Before this disease, I never even thought of my saliva. I unconsciously swallowed it when there was too much in my mouth. You don't even realize that you have a lot of saliva. Now however, I don't swallow as much as before and without medication there is a great surplus in the quantities of saliva. That is why it began going down the wrong way.

While saliva is useful in the digestive process when food is ingested through the mouth, for me it is my worst enemy. I have to be able to control it. I was successful in doing this for about a week, but my body got used to the drugs, and started producing more saliva. I was coughing because of it. For a time I thought I had the problem solved but it became a problem again.

Now I am using more of the medication to control my saliva, and I think I am getting it under control again. Increasing the dosage of my anti-saliva medication might not be the answer yet. I have had two more actions that might be a permanent help for this situation.

A test was done using radiation to see if my saliva is actually going into my lungs. I know that some has done this at times. However, the saliva test didn't prove it. The type of pneumonia that I have gotten does not have anything to do with a cold. My lungs have just gotten plugged up. X-rays do not even show pneumonia. That is why it is considered to be aspirating pneumonia. Now that I eat very little food, the main goal is for me not to produce much saliva to hopefully avoid aspirating pneumonia.

Also, there is the possibility that I will get radiation treatments done to close some of my saliva glands. Hopefully this will reduce the problems that I have had, and perhaps I can even stop taking some anti-saliva medication. This is a new procedure for A.L.S. patients. It has been done for some who suffer with cancer, but I will be one of the first A.L.S. patients in Canada to have it done. These changes that I have to adjust to are taking place quite rapidly.

Getting Used To Changes in My Body

This is one of the biggest problems that I face. Before this disease I was in fairly good condition. It is true that I weighed too much and losing some weight was a blessing. I was exercising regularly and I could carry heavy objects around and move quite quickly without it bothering me.

The last trip to the hospital seemed to do a number on me. I was really quite weak afterwards, which was the expectation. I had a severe case of pneumonia, I hadn't eaten for five of those ten days, and I generally felt weak. I was still coughing when I came out and it took about a week to gain control of my saliva and clear up the coughing.

Once I stopped coughing I got some strength back - but it wasn't like it was before. When I was healthy, I could regain my strength quite quickly. With ALS, you never get all your strength back once you lose it. You have so much energy to use in a day, and you won't get back what you use.

That is a change that I am not really ready to accept. I have taken up walking for half an hour, three or four days a week. This has been enjoyable. They really haven't tired me out. However, my strength has not returned as it once did. Somehow I think having a PEG in my stomach reduces my ability to regain all of my strength. I don't know if that is true, but I do know that I don't have the strength that I once had.

The cough seems to come back periodically even though I have no lung infection. It is a hard problem to overcome. However, I have discovered from the A.L.S. Manual another reason for the cough. From that manual we read:

You may find that tube feeding causes excessive coughing. This may happen for a number of reasons, including excess saliva, not sitting up enough, the feeding rate is too fast, or because of various other stomach problems.[8]

This demonstrates to me that it isn't always aspiration that causes me to cough. There are other matters to consider.

It is true that coughing brings more saliva into my mouth so it is a vicious circle to deal with. Coughing also reduces my strength and some days when I am coughing I just do not feel very good. My body is not working as it should. Even though I don't have pain to speak of, coughing makes me uncomfortable. I always have a handkerchief with me when I am coughing.

My lungs are quite sensitive now because of the bouts that I have had with pneumonia. Dr. Myrholm has prescribed some antibiotics that I can start using if my lungs get any more infection in them. If I am coughing a lot, we will be calling our respiratory therapist or our nurse practitioner to come and check my lungs out. If there is an infection in my lungs, I will start using the medication right away.

With my lungs being so sensitive, I need to stay away from people who have colds. I cannot go outside when it is inclement. I hope that walking will strengthen my lungs. However, if the disease is moving to my lungs, they may not be able to improve very much. I seem to get lung infections from time to time, but I am thankful to Dr. Myrholm and others who find it quickly enough before it develops into pneumonia.

Care for my mouth and throat has become another issue since I have stopped using it for eating and drinking. Besides have the "furry mouth", I also have been bothered by "strep throat". That was relatively painful until Dr. Myrholm got me on some medication, which cleaned it up quickly. I also have medicated mouthwash that I take four times a day. My mouth is quite clean now, even though my specialist (Dr. Kalra) says that saliva is very dirty and can cause infection if it is not reduced. I am adjusting to the care for my mouth.

My tongue really needs brushing to get the bacteria off of it and because nerves there start doing some weird things. Sometimes I feel that my mouth is filled with little pieces of things that apparently come from

[8] "Living With ALS, page 52

my stomach. Brushing my tongue and applying medication helps to make it feel much cleaner.

Sleeping on My Own Adjustable Bed

There are a few reasons for why it is difficult for me to sleep on a flat bed. Firstly, according to the latest tests, I do not exhale all my carbon dioxide unless my head is elevated. However I had to have an elevated front to my bed long before the latest results.

An elevated front was to help me to breathe properly and to stop saliva from going into my lungs. I also need the head of my bed elevated because if I sleep with my bed flat, the food could come from my stomach up to my throat.

When Ann talked to the A.L.S. Director about the need for an adjustable bed, one was found and brought to our place almost immediately. We are very grateful for that. It has a very good mattress that is better than you'd find on a hospital bed. It can be raised up from the front and the back by remote control and I only elevate the front to about thirty degrees. It is a single bed, which means that my wife and I sleep separately.

Sleeping in a separate bed from my wife is very different. We have been sleeping together for almost thirty-eight years, and have enjoyed each other's company. So this has been quite an adjustment. I miss that we do not sleep together. We sit together to have prayer before we go to sleep. I used to always lead in prayer, but now it is hard for me to pray aloud so Ann leads.

It takes me longer to prepare for bed. I need to take some medication, and then brush my teeth and my tongue, rinse my mouth out and take the medicated mouthwash.

I regularly have problems getting to sleep. Sometimes I am coughing, but other times I just seem to be keyed up and cannot sleep properly. A good sleep means that I only wake up a couple of times and am able to get back to sleep right away. There is enough nights where I don't get adequate sleep and so new measures will be taken.

The other thing happens when I read my Bible for the best part of an hour in the mornings. Sometimes I have to fight to concentrate and keep my eyes open. For most of my life I would get up at 6:00 A.M. for devotions and never have the kinds of problems that I have now. I am tired early in the morning. The fatigue is good evidence that I am not expelling my carbon dioxide.

However, a test was recently taken to determine the amount of carbon dioxide in my blood stream. That test came out very well in that the carbon dioxide wasn't there as suspected. However, there were other reasons for me to get the biPap machine, including the last pulmonary test.

I have recently learned that if I am really tired in the mornings while I am having my devotions, that I should just have a nap. On the few occasions that I have tried that, I have been able to sleep for an hour and awaken much more refreshed.

The Cost of Medications

Previously when I was principal at Three Hills, we were on a group plan with which all medications were covered up to 80% as well as visits to the dentist, and other coverage that we needed. When the company learned of my preexisting condition they no longer would allow us to have the same kind of benefits that we had before. The individual plan they offered us was expensive and did not cover very much. The government has a health plan for terminally ill patients that will cover 70% of the medications. We are very grateful for the government program covering the medication but without the extended benefits, it meant a significant change in coverage for us.

The big problem came up when I left the hospital in January. We had prescriptions for a large amount of medication. For example in the month of February, we paid two hundred dollars for my medication. On a limited budget that we now have, it was quite a lot of money to put out. We are hoping that can be changed soon, because it can be very costly for us.

Though I do not have the coverage that I would like, it does seem that there is enough assistance for me, which I am happy about. But I am also thinking of others who may have terminal diseases and actually use more medication than I do. You probably have bigger concerns, so I guess that I shouldn't complain.

The Ability to Travel

Ann and I have always enjoyed traveling. We thought that as we got older and retired, we would like to travel a great deal - including visiting missionaries around the world. However, the illness kind of throws a monkey wrench into our plans.

I really don't even know if I will be around when Ann is ready to retire. The time frame for the disease shows that I might be dead within the next five years or so. But we must remember that it is God Who is in control. He is the One Who gives life and takes it away. He may give me several more years to live. It all depends upon what He plans for my future.

The Desire to Visit Our Son and Family in New Zealand

As I mentioned previously, our son Trevor and his wife Karen and family have recently felt that God has called them to New Zealand to minister there. They have discovered that New Zealand is quite different from Canada in terms of finding a ministry and a place to work. Their children are in a Christian school now, which is good, but they have to make adjustments because the school year is different. Trevor and Karen are still exploring what they should be doing. A ministry will open up for Trevor but it will take some time for that to develop.

We would definitely like to visit them in New Zealand because we have never been away from North America. We would also like to give them some support, helping them out in any way. We often receive emails from them, including video and audio messages. Often the children especially will say that they miss us and would like us to come to see them. Being very close to our family means that it is very difficult when one moves halfway around the world.

We are actually at the point of considering if we should go see them, but a decision like that depends a great deal upon my health. I would have to be good for a period of time before I could go so I would not have to be concerned about contracting pneumonia. My immune system needs to be strengthened. Once my body is stabilized, I would think that we should be able to go. However, there are a lot of other considerations that we must include.

Changes Needed in Travelling

There are quite a few plans needed if we were to travel any distance. It certainly is not as simple as it was before. Even last Christmas, when we decided to go to Los Angeles as a holiday for everyone in our family, there was a tremendous amount of things to consider.

There were only certain foods that I could eat. I had a lot of scrambled eggs for breakfast! We went to a restaurant that had a good-sized salad bar and I was able to get soup and a lot of other small foods that I could eat without choking. We went to the Medieval Times where the only food given was chicken and spare ribs. We brought a portable grinder along and ground up the food manually. It took a lot of time to do this and the meat got very dry. We had considered buying a power grinder when we got home so that we could go to restaurants and grind up the meal. However, God had other things in mind since I soon ended up in the hospital and came out not being able to eat foods through my mouth. Actually I lost about six pounds on our trip to California, and lost a lot more when I was in the hospital.

On our last trip, I could at least eat some regular food. However any further trips would not allow that. Now I would have to feed myself through the tube. That means I would have to pack my cans of food along with me.

I consume 6.5 cans per day and there are 24 cans in a case. That means I go through one case every three days with two feedings on the fourth day. In one week I need 45.5 cans and for three weeks I would need 136.5 cans - about six cases of food. Each case weighs about 14 pounds so I would have to bring 84 pounds. That would be quite heavy to carry around, and it would be interesting to get that through customs! I am not sure how we can do that at this stage but obviously we would have to make some provision. It is possible that some food could be purchased there or we could make arrangements for the food to be available.

The medication would have to come along and if I was going on a long holiday overseas I would probably have to stock up refills. All of these are in plastic containers that could not be thrown around. We would make them part of our carry-on luggage. All of these considerations are important to me since I could not travel without them.

I would be bringing along syringes for medication and water. I could use a sixty-milliliter syringe for feeding myself. That way I wouldn't need the bag and tubing along that I use for gravity feeding. I would need about five syringes full for each meal with some delays in between, but that would work out not too badly.

For sleeping I definitely need the front of my bed raised. We have an 18-inch wedge that may work but that is also a very cumbersome parcel to pack. I might just settle for getting extra pillows to prop up with. That might work for me. When I tried it before, I slept not too badly and I expect that would still be the case.

Trevor and Karen returned back home from New Zealand in August and so our desire to visit them there has vanished. Trevor actually helped a great deal with the publication of this book, so he has been an invaluable help to me at home.

We can probably travel by car with little difficulty, and perhaps we will be doing that sort of thing.

Problems with Swimming

On holidays we like to go to a resort with a swimming pool or a beach where we can have fun with our grandchildren. This is something that we do almost every year with one or more of our children, but now swimming is really out of the question for me. Other activities might still occur but great care has to be taken.

It would be difficult for me to wear a bathing suit without a top on because of the PEG in my stomach. I probably would not dare to go in water with my PEG because of the dangers of infection that might come. Even going to swim at a lake would be out of the question. Infections both inside and out are things that I need to be very careful about. There are many changes in my body and unless the Lord heals me, vacations will be much more complicated.

Other Reasons Why Travel Might Be Difficult

I suppose that my biggest concern should be to stay alive. Travel will be quite limited because of the progression of the disease. Time is running out. We cannot plan on traveling too far into the future because we don't know what it will hold. I know that if the Lord takes me home, my trip to heaven will be the greatest trip that I could ever take so I shouldn't be too concerned about not being able to travel much now!

There is also the problem of gaining insurance when traveling. If we traveled within Canada it probably would not be a problem. However, it may be more of a problem if we travel outside of the country to New Zealand. These are areas that we will have to look through when planning a trip.

You see from this chapter that there are many changes because of the disease. On the one hand I feel good enough to travel some, but on the other hand I have to be careful in what I do because my body is much more sensitive than it was before. Unless my resistance builds up, I could be susceptible to infection very easily. So I continue to need God's strength in my life!

Chapter Six:
Faith Versus Acceptance

I want to spend some time in discussing how I approached this disease because this was an important factor for me. It has been very difficult to be continually full of faith and believing God will heal when there has been so much that has gone wrong with my body. By the way I am very grateful that I still have the use of my hands and my feet. God has been good to me in many ways, regardless of the fact that I haven't been healed yet. However, I hovered between faith and acceptance for quite awhile.

Accepting the Sentence of Death

I remember a certain individual. He was a person who believed that he would die soon, regardless of how healthy he seemed to be at the time. He had accepted Christ as his Saviour. Eventually he did obtain a rapid moving form of cancer, and put his faith into the fact that he would die soon. Well he did die. What he had believed came to pass.

I didn't go quite as far as he did, but I was accepting the probability of dying with this fatal disease. And like his condition, it is progressing very quickly. For quite a while I was thinking of heaven as a great place to go in order to escape this world and this body. I was accepting this disease, thinking that God was ready to take me home. That to me is the easy way out – a way that leads to eternal life. I had lived a pretty good life, and that was only a prelude to what would come later.

As I indicated previously, a time came in devotions when I realized that it was Satan who was behind this illness, and it was Satan who wanted me to have this temptation, thinking that I would give up believing that God would heal me. I wrote this in my memoirs on October 14, 2004:

> "This idea of not living very long has been impressed on me quite forcefully over the last few days, and I know that if God does not undertake for me, that I will go to be with Him very shortly. I was feeling that this might not be too bad, but today I came to the conclusion that I do not want to die because of something

Satan put upon me. I would rather die when God felt that I had finished my course and that I had accomplished all that He wanted me to do. At age 58, I don't know if I have accomplished all that I would like to do yet! I feel I could minister to others a great deal yet, especially to get them ready for Christ's return. Therefore I am expecting that God will heal me!"[9]

After that day, I changed my thinking considerably. I now desire to be healed by God because I feel that I can be useful to Him in the future. Now I am ready for a battle, though my body feels very weak and my will is probably not a strong as it should be. As far as my body is concerned, I don't feel any victory at this point. However, I feel that what I need to do is to grow in faith.

Growing in Faith

It is one thing to have faith, but when you have a deadly disease it is hard to really take command over your illness and believe that God is definitely going to heal you. Others have professed that sort of faith towards me, but somehow I haven't grasped it fully.

However as I read the scriptures, I see that it is my own responsibility to grow in faith. *"But you, dear friends, build yourselves up in your most holy faith and pray in the Holy Spirit. Keep yourselves in God's love as you wait for the mercy of our Lord Jesus Christ to bring you to eternal life."* (Jude 20, 21) We see here that it is our own responsibility to grow in faith. And how do we grow in faith? We see the answer here: *"Consequently, faith comes from hearing the message, and the message is heard through the word of Christ,"* (Romans 10:17). Therefore it is important for me to study the Word of God, but also need to hear it preached regularly. I have heard some very good messages concerning healing on television recently. But I have to keep immersed in the Word regularly. I also need to go through the scriptures on healing on a regular basis. I have to build myself up in faith!

Reading books about healing can be very useful also, for they can increase a person's faith. I hope you can see that this is truly a "fight of faith," having the kind of faith that can guarantee healing as my goal. At the same time I have to be ready to fight against the powers of darkness that are arrayed against me.

---

[9] "Thoughts Regarding a Fatal Disease", page 19

During my devotions on November 25, 2004 I felt that God was telling me something important that I will share that with you at this time:

> In my devotions today, I felt that God was telling me that I should have faith that He is going to heal me. I remember that with my back problems, it took quite awhile before I was healed from that problem. So I feel that I simply have to have faith that the healing process will begin when God feels I have enough faith to believe that He will heal me. Rather than accepting death (which is okay for me), I should be thinking instead of healing and then I can be a greater witness for my Lord. I think that in the next 15 or 20 years I could be pretty effective in serving Him.[10]

It is my desire to remain alive and to have my body healed because I feel that I could truly be effective for Him in the days ahead. I must fight the fight of faith and believe in the great miracle it would be if God was to heal me. I do believe that He will perform that miracle in my life! When He does that it is completely up to Him.

The writings of Paul are important in this thought of having faith or simply accepting death because of this fatal disease. On the one hand it is good to be with Jesus, but on the other hand, I could be effective for the Lord if I was healed.

The Example of Paul

I have some of the same views that Paul expressed in writing to the Philippians:

> *For to me, to live is Christ and to die is gain. If I am to go on living in the body, this will mean fruitful labour for me. Yet what shall I choose? I do not know! I am torn between the two: I desire to depart and be with Christ, which is better by far; but it is more necessary for you that I remain in the body. Convinced of this, I know that I will remain, and I will continue with all of you for your progress and joy in the faith, so that through my being with you again your joy in Christ Jesus will overflow on account of me.*
> (Philippians 1:20 – 26)

---

[10] "Thoughts Regarding a Fatal Disease", page 26

We see that Paul felt it would be advantageous to the people if he were to remain, even though it would be better for him to go. Paul was torn between the two options, and I feel the same as he felt. On the one hand, heaven would be a much better place for me to be because I would be free from a body that is quickly deteriorating. It is not pleasant for me to live in it any longer. In heaven I would have a new body! If God was to heal me, I would still be in this body but it would be a much better place to dwell. I do not think that it could be considered a lack of faith to want to go to heaven. However, it does take faith to believe that God is going to heal me.

Obviously it would be better for Ann and our family if I remained on earth and I also feel that I can be very useful to God even at this stage of my life. You can see that there is an important decision in this. If I simply accept the disease that has been put upon me, one day I will die and go to be with Jesus. That would be a tremendous reward for me. But on the other hand, if I exercise faith that God is going to heal me a great fight is ahead. Paul, in giving instructions to Timothy, wrote:

> *Timothy, my son, I give you this instruction in keeping with the prophecies once made about you, so that by following them you may fight the good fight, holding on to faith and a good conscience. Some have rejected these and so have shipwrecked their faith.* (1 Timothy 1: 18, 19)

Timothy was encouraged to "hold on to faith and a good conscience." In other words, his task was to exercise faith in the most difficult situation. To him it was a fight of faith, and I am in that same position. I have to fight the good fight in order to see God's healing come to pass. If I simply rejected God because of His delay in healing me, I could be counted as one who has "shipwrecked his faith." I have no intention on doing that. I will continue to serve God whether I live or die.

Prophecies Made Over Me

In the scripture above, Paul commented that Timothy's ministry really began with the prophecies made over him. He was to use those prophecies to help him to "fight the good fight." An interesting event happened at Pastor's Camp last summer (August, 2004). My wife and I were called forward and several pastors gathered around for prayer. Several prophecies were given. I had put them into my memoirs as soon as we returned home. I give them to you just as I remembered what was said. I cannot remember who said what, but these are messages that were given to them from God.

"God sees what you are going through and is with you."

"Just as you put salt on a snail to kill it and just as it takes some time for the snail to die, so what Satan has put on you will take some time to die, but the power of God will eventually be victorious. You will be eventually free of the tormenter's work."

A young boy came with a vision of "the Spirit coming over you as water flooding over you from heaven."

Another pastor stated, "Just as a dam can stop the flow of water, so your speech has been dammed up for a little while. However, the dam will soon be broken, and a mighty river will ensue. Your speech will come back."

A pastor spoke of Zachariah, the priest, who was told by an angel that he would have a son. Zachariah's speech was taken away, but it returned when he wrote that the child's name would be John. Zachariah then brought forth a powerful prophecy: (Luke 1:68-79). "In the same way after some time, your voice will return and you will have a powerful ministry."

Another said: "God is holding something in His hand, which for a time will withhold the answer from you. However, God would soon open His hand with deliverance and you will be free."

"Put your toes into the rippling stream of the Holy Spirit. As you step out into deeper water, God's blessing will be upon you."

"I will be with you in the valley and walk with you. And I will make your feet as hind's feet upon the high mountains. You will be swift and sure. You will be able to run on the crags without falling."[11]

I take these prophecies as coming directly from God. Notice the several messages that spoke of my healing coming after some time had passed. I believe that these should be reason enough for me to "fight the good fight of faith"! I believe that victory is on the way. In a later chapter I will speak about having victory regardless of the outcome but here I will state that I am looking for victory in the physical as well as in the spiritual realm. Satan will be defeated. Many of these prophecies are very special to me, as I hope they are with you.

I have several reasons for believing that God is going to heal me. He spoke through other pastors to give me this news. Therefore I must be obedient to Him and believe that He will touch me in a miraculous way soon.

I have to confess that there has been times, especially when my body has been very upset, when I have thought that death would be the best way to be free. Then I have to remind myself that I have God's promises before me, and that He is faithful to keep His Word.

God's faithfulness never fails us. Here is a verse of scripture that shows just about where I feel I am, but it also shows how God is always there to help. *"A bruised reed He will not break, and a smoldering wick He will not snuff out. In faithfulness He will bring forth justice."* (Isaiah 42:3) God is a God of love and faithfulness! He is faithful to keep His Word, even though He hasn't healed me yet. I believe that He will be faithful to His promises within His Word.

The Demonstration of Faith

Some people say that to demonstrate faith, you have to do something that you could not do before. In other words you have to put out a fleece to show God that you are standing on your faith. What is it that I could not do? Should I go to the front of the church we attend and claim that God has healed me? That would be a problem because people cannot understand what I am saying. I really don't know if there is anything I could do to demonstrate my faith - at this time, anyway.

---

[11] "Thoughts Regarding a Fatal Disease", page 5

I guess that all I can really do is express faith in the fact that God is going to heal me. If I go to my death bed with this faith that is okay. Meanwhile, I have to concentrate on something else that God talked to me about as I was reading the book of Philippians:

I rejoice greatly in the Lord that at last you have renewed your concern for me. Indeed, you have been concerned, but you had no opportunity to show it. I am not saying this because I am in need, for I have learned to be content whatever the circumstances. I know what it is to be in need, and I know what it is to have plenty. I have learned the secret of being content in any and every situation, whether well fed or hungry, whether living in plenty or in want. I can do everything through Him who gives me strength. (Phil. 4:10-13)

I have to learn to be content in my situation. For the most part I can say that I haven't complained much, though you might think that is the case in Chapter Four. I do feel though, that it is good to ask God questions when things are not going the way you want them to go. Just take a look at the Psalms for example.

This can be a real frustration sometimes, especially when excess saliva is making me cough and making me feel very uncomfortable. I suppose that I need to work at being content in every situation. God pointed this scripture out to me recently in my devotions.

I know that it is important to have the mindset that God is going to heal me, and not to focus on the thoughts that He might not do so. If I have such a mindset, I need to make plans for the future. What it really means is that I will be able to finish writing both of my books and even more books. He possibly would use me to talk to many others in churches to demonstrate that He has healed me. While I cannot talk right now, I can write. Therefore I have to do what I can to bring praise to my God.

I need to have the kind of faith that Jesus talked about:

Jesus replied, "I tell you the truth, if you have faith and do not doubt, not only can you do what was done to the fig tree, but also you can say to this mountain, 'Go, throw yourself into the sea,' and it will be done." (Matthew 21:21)

This is tremendous faith to have, and I would say that if I had this kind of faith, I would be victorious over this disease. I must have faith and not doubt. As you read this book, you can see where I am at right now. Hopefully I will continue to grow in faith and be able to demonstrate that faith. This needs to be my goal.

How to Fight the Good Fight

It is also very interesting that one verse of scripture that came out many times was from Isaiah's writings: *"No weapon forged against you will prevail, and you will refute every tongue that accuses you. This is the heritage of the servants of the LORD, and this is their vindication from Me,' declares the LORD."* (Isaiah 54:17) This is a wonderful promise to embrace when we are fighting the good fight of faith. About three people thought of the same verse at the same time, including my wife, my daughter and a friend.

As well, when my wife phoned Joyce Meyer's Ministry to ask for prayer, she was put on hold for a few minutes and the music that came over the phone was a song based on that verse. The fight has very solid ground against our enemy, the devil. As long as I can keep expressing faith that God is going to heal me, the devil does not have anything to stand on as we claim this verse in our fight of faith.

It is good to be able to be involved in this kind of a fight. But admittedly it has been quite difficult for me to be consistent in it. I have been considering what I have to do to be able to fight the good fight and how I can enter into spiritual warfare against Satan. These could be one and the same tasks.

I have to fight in order to have the kind of faith that I need. However to really win the war, I have to enter into spiritual warfare. This is something that in my present condition I have not been good at. For example it is hard to get deep into prayer when I am coughing. Honestly though, I need to discipline myself enough so that I can concentrate on the task at hand.

We find some comments about this spiritual warfare in the following passage:

> *Finally, be strong in the Lord and in his mighty power. Put on the full armour of God so that you can take your stand against the devil's schemes. For our struggle is not against flesh and blood, but against the rulers, against the authorities, against the powers of this dark world and against the spiritual forces of evil in the heavenly realms.* (Eph.6:10-12)

We need to have the wisdom to protect ourselves from the schemes of the devil. The irony of the rest of the passage is that faith is probably the greatest component of our spiritual armour – the "shield of faith." We need faith before we can enter into any spiritual conflict. Our enemy is pointed out very clearly. It is not people, even though people might be involved in it at times. It is spiritual forces of evil that are planning for my destruction.

The passage above talks about being "strong in the Lord." I have to confess that in this condition I don't feel strong like I often did in the past. I have seen several spiritual victories over the years. I rely upon God for the strength that He has given me. He gives me strength every day, and I believe that strength helps me to live in a victorious manner. However, I need to have an even greater amount of strength to be able in Christ to defeat the powers of our enemy.

I certainly thank God for the individuals who are involved in spiritual warfare on my behalf. However, I am at the stage where I don't feel I can sit on the sidelines and watch others being involved in this war without actively getting involved myself. It is obvious that a spiritual stronghold has put this condition upon me and it needs to be broken. We see how this battle is spelled out in the spiritual realm from God's Word:

> *For though we live in the world, we do not wage war as the world does. The weapons we fight with are not the weapons of the world. On the contrary, they have divine power to demolish strongholds. We demolish arguments and every pretension that sets itself up against the knowledge of God, and we take captive every thought to make it obedient to Christ.*
> (2 Corinthians 10:3-5)

The warfare takes place in the minds of people who allow views contrary to the knowledge God grants. It is the devil that puts those false ideas into their minds. To a certain extent it has happened to me, because I find it difficult to concentrate while I am in prayer. Confusing thoughts that I have are not from God but from the enemy. I need to be rebuking the enemy for putting such thoughts into my head. This is definitely something that I need to work on. But it's a struggle because our physical being is exploited by the enemy to affect our spiritual being.

Fighting against spiritual forces that are invading my life is not playtime. It is extremely serious, and takes a great deal of spiritual energy. It is a war! I need the spiritual strength that God can give me so that I can be successful in prayer. The need for spiritual power is great. Paul prayed for this power to be on God's people in a marvellous way: "*I pray that out of His glorious riches He may strengthen you with power through His Spirit in your inner being,*"(Ephesians 3:16). I certainly need God to answer that prayer on my behalf! He has all of the power and authority to do that, so I hope that it will happen in spite of what this illness has done to me.

There is another promise of God that means a great deal. It is the promise that He will strengthen us, as we believe Him for that. *"So do not fear, for I am with you; do not be dismayed, for I am your God. I will strengthen you and help you; I will uphold you with my righteous right hand."* (Isaiah 41:10) I believe His promises, and I believe that He will strengthen me. Praise His name!

We also gain spiritual strength from prayer, as long as we can wait upon Him. Isaiah has another popular verse in which he describes how we can get strength. *"Yet those who wait for the LORD will gain new strength; they will mount up with wings like eagles, they will run and not get tired, they will walk and not become weary."* (Isaiah 40:31 NASB) We need to spend a considerable amount of time in prayer before we gain the victory talked about in this verse. This is the kind of strength that I need today – strength to fly over this illness and run without getting weary. Today if I walk up the stairs too many times I get extremely tired. It would be a blessing not to get tired. If I wait on the Lord I will gain my healing in Him. God, please help me to spend more time in prayer and in Your presence!

There is another verse of scripture I want to share. Hopefully I can be able to say this is absolutely true, because I will have won the war when I can make this profession: *"You armed me with strength for battle; You made my adversaries bow at my feet."* (2 Samuel 22:40) I depend upon God to arm me with strength for the battle, and I would love to see my enemies (demons) bowing at my feet. May God strengthen me with His marvellous power!

I trust you can see the kinds of battles a believer must be involved in order to defeat our common enemy. The biggest thing that I need on a daily basis is God's strength so that I can fight those battles. Through the verses that I have quoted here, gaining His power should not be that difficult. What is most difficult is the tearing down of strongholds in my mind so that I can be more effective in prayer. Once I can wait upon the Lord on a daily basis, I believe that my strength will be renewed.

I should reiterate that God has been very close to me throughout this time and He has given me the strength to go through each day with a good attitude. I am not down too much these days in spite of the deterioration of my body. But for eventual healing to take place, I know that the enemy's power has to be broken. That only happens as we fight the good fight of faith and come out victorious because God is on our side!

Believing the Promises of God

Immersing myself in the Word of God is what gives me strength from day to day. Since August 2004 to the end of March, 2005 I have read the Bible through in its entirety. I read the Bible for almost one hour per day, and I take time to meditate on verses that are promises or examples of how God has helped others. I have regularly felt that power that comes from the Word of God. It gives me the strength to go through what I have been going through. It takes a large amount of prayer to break the powers of darkness and gain the victory over such an illness.

I would like to share some more of those promises with you. I have in mind others who are going through similar trials with only death in sight and their caregivers who will be encouraged by these promises. These are what I go through on a daily basis in addition to reading the Bible. We find the first verse from the Psalms: "*O LORD my God, I called to You for help and You healed me.*" (Psalm 30:2) This is a promise that came true for David. God had healed him from some infirmity. When David asked for His help, God healed him. I believe that He should do the same for me as well. It is a promise that I claim.

The next portion I want to share with you is from an anonymous psalm – we do not know who wrote it. However, it has been very special to me because in many ways it parallels my life. I love the way the writer describes the troubles he has had, but then also the faith that he has that from the depths of the earth God will raise him up again.

> *Your righteousness reaches to the skies, O God, You who have done great things. Who, O God, is like You? Though You have made me see troubles, many and bitter, You will restore my life again; from the depths of the earth You will again bring me up. You will increase my honor and comfort me once again.* (Psalm 71:19-21)

I am in the depths of the earth with this illness, and I also believe that God will raise me up again. This is a great passage of scripture though it doesn't specifically talk of healing. Truly because God is such a great God who has done great things, He can do this for me as well. His righteousness does reach to the skies, and He is faithful to keep His Word. Praise His Name!

David wrote a psalm that is often used by pastors around Thanksgiving Sunday. Part of it includes a section on healing that I am giving to you here. *"Praise the LORD, O my soul, and forget not all His benefits - Who forgives all your sins and heals all your diseases, who redeems your life from the pit and crowns you with love and compassion."* (Psalm 103:2 – 4)

We need to bring praise to our God, for He does give us wonderful benefits. It is marvellous to be able to serve such a loving God who heals all of our diseases. Through Christ's blood He has redeemed us, and that is the most important gift we receive from Him. That is why I can say that I have no fear of death at all, because He has redeemed me from the pit. I feel His love each and every day, and I am sure that His compassion will be shown very clearly when He heals me. Since this passage says that He heals all our diseases, I know He will heal me as well. One health worker told our family that she has not seen anyone healed from A.L.S. I would like to be the first, and others can follow me as well!

> *Then they cried to the LORD in their trouble, and He saved them from their distress. He sent forth His word and healed them; He rescued them from the grave. Let them give thanks to the LORD for His unfailing love and His wonderful deeds for men.* (Psalm 107:19 – 21)

I, and many others, have called for the Lord's help in our trouble, and have found the Lord faithful to save us from our distress. Just as He sent forth His word and healed us, I believe that He will do that once again for me. That is one reason why I spend so much time in the Word, although I love the Word regardless of my condition. If He heals me He will very definitely rescue my life from the grave.

I do praise You O God for all that You do for us from day to day. Truly You are a great God!

In Isaiah 53 we have Isaiah predicting the death of Christ about seven hundred years before it took place. He was truly a tremendous prophet who spoke with exactness and spoke more of the coming Redeemer than anyone else did. Here is one verse that relates to my healing. *"But He was pierced for our transgressions, He was crushed for our iniquities; the punishment that brought us peace was upon Him, and by His wounds we are healed."* (Isaiah 53:5) Because of what Jesus did for us on the Cross our healing should be guaranteed. With those wounds that He bore for us, our sins are atoned for, but they also give us the ability to be healed.

Isaiah has another verse concerning healing that I cherish a great deal. *"Then your light will break forth like the dawn, and your healing will quickly appear; then your righteousness One will go before you, and the glory of the LORD will be your rear guard."* (Isaiah 58:8) This speaks to me as though my healing will come suddenly as "my light" breaks through. I am anticipating a sudden and complete healing; that is what I am praying for.

I have so many other verses that I love and meditate upon every day. I simply don't have the room to give you all of them. I will give you one more, but bear in mind that I have not even touched the New Testament where there are several verses demonstrating how Christ *"went about doing good,"* (Acts 10:38). The following verse shows the reaction that people might have after they have been healed, and I would think that this would cause me great joy as well! *"But for you who revere My name, the sun of righteousness will rise with healing in its wings. And you will go out and leap like calves released from the stall."* (Malachi 4:2) Being raised on a farm, I can remember how frisky young calves can be. If I was totally healed, there would be tremendous rejoicing over God's goodness to me. In anticipation of my healing, I will praise Him for it even now!

I have given you seven passages out of nine pages of promises that I meditate upon as many as five days every week. These verses have become very precious promises to me that I can stand upon with regards to my healing. A faithful God will honour His Word, and will I believe, heal my body. This is a great way to meditate upon God's Word. I encourage you to do something similar so that His Word is before you all of the time. God is good and He is faithful to His Word!

Chapter Seven:

Personal Feelings Regarding My Condition

Though I have shared some of my feelings regarding this disease throughout this book, it may be beneficial to focus more on them in this chapter. The changes in my body have caused some great changes in my thinking. This has happened so quickly that it takes me quite awhile to adjust.

For example, the first night after I left the hospital I had a whole bunch of medications that I had to take through my feeding tube. I think there were about eighteen different syringes of drugs that I had to take throughout the week. While in the hospital I was taught how to give myself the feedings, but I hadn't yet attempted the medications. I understood that I needed to have water after each drug. Well, it turned out that I took way too much water and my tube opened itself four times in less than half an hour. The contents of my stomach sprayed onto the floor. I lost all the medication. I knew I had to adjust.

We also had to figure out how much of each medication I needed to take. It took well over a half an hour just to fill my syringes. We knew this would be a headache so Ann phoned the Home Care nurse. She brought several smaller syringes that would be more suitable for various drugs and she showed Ann how to prepare them. Our daughter Janine made up a chart on the computer so that I could check off what I took. Using three cups to put filled syringes into, everything would be prepared before I had to take the medication. The system worked very well. Eventually I began using two cups because the amount of medications had dropped off considerably. Now I prepare everything for myself.

The amount of medication I need to take often depends on how I have been feeling. For example, I have to take blood pressure medication - though my blood pressure is getting much better since I have lost so much weight. From time to time I get infections in my lungs, or strep throat, or gout. This always means that more medications are needed. At bedtime I usually take some medication and prune juice to get my bowels working. I initially had two different medications that I took to control my saliva, but now with two sets of radiation done for me, I don't take any. Now I prepare my drugs without even needing any papers. I know everything because I have been taking it so often, and I fill up the syringe with the next medication before I start the feeding. It is working very well, but it took some time to adjust to it. Of course, I was a bit frustrated with the entire process until I adjusted to it. This is just one example of the feelings I have had to deal with. I have many others that I would like to share with you at this time.

Feelings of Loneliness Despite the Support

There are many times that I feel desperately lonely in spite of the very strong support that I get from my family and the professional health workers. The strange thing is that I feel most lonely when I am in a group such as a birthday party for a member of our family. There is good food for everyone that I cannot partake of, and there are a lot of conversations that I usually cannot be involved in.

Though I am there, it seems that I really am not part of the group. I feel lonely because it is difficult for me to contribute to conversations or eat the food that everyone else is eating. This might seem strange, but it is very real. It can end up being a very miserable time for me.

I take my voice synthesizer with me to almost every function these days. However, it is hard to keep up with the conversation when you have to type in what you want to say. By the time I finish typing often the subject has been changed. It is better for me to have one-on-one conversations with people, because then they wait for me to type out what I want to say.

I almost always have to use the synthesizer now, because even my wife cannot understand what I am saying. When I don't have it along, I use a piece of paper to write on. The voice synthesizer does not compare with ordinary conversation, and at times I just remain quiet and don't bother saying anything.

Please understand that this doesn't have anything to do with the people I gather with. In fact many people, when they see me typing, will say, "Howard has something to say." They do want to include me in their conversation, and that is good. However, I feel that I just don't fit in such situations.

I should underscore the fact that I am always aware of God's presence with me, so I should never feel lonely. God is always with me, but I feel His presence more when I am on my own. So when I say that I feel lonely, I am lonely because I cannot relate well to people who are all around me. God does ease the pain of loneliness.

I recently found that I feel much better when I am included in playing a game. Then I feel part of the group and I am more satisfied with coming. I love my family very much and want to be present when they have birthday parties and other gatherings.

I don't know what can be done. Everyone wants me to be there even though I am limited in what I say. But I become alienated in crowds. So sometimes I want to be alone.

The Desire to be Left Alone

Related to the last problem of feeling lonely is the feeling of wanting to be alone. I am never lonely if I am by myself. I suppose that is because I am busy all of the time. But being alone also means I don't have to try to get someone to understand me - unless I get a phone call.

And it means that I can "do my own thing." I can be busy writing books. I enjoy watching sports such as baseball, football, hockey, or golf on television, but I seldom take the time to watch the entire game. I am happy to be able to keep busy, because my spirits keep high when I am.

I have found that I must pace myself. I cannot do too much physical activity because I get tired out pretty quickly. I also cannot be standing for a long time because that will give me a sore back or legs. Still, I like to get my exercise every day. I walk pretty fast so I take a walk at least three times a week. I'd rather do it five times, but often I've got other things to do.

Part of the reason why I prefer being alone is because when I am alone I don't care about being different. I always carry my handkerchief with me so that if I start coughing I can stop the saliva. That is not always easy to do in a public area. However, no one will be looking at me or feeling sorry for me when I am alone. Therefore it is quite satisfying to be alone at times.

I know that if the Lord does not heal me, my body could be degenerating to the place where I will need to be supervised for twenty-four hours a day. I certainly hope that I never get to that but in the meantime, I appreciate the times that I can have for myself.

My wife Ann is quite different. Not knowing how much time I have left, Ann likes to be with me as much as possible. I understand her and so try to help her as much as I can. She is very special to me - even more so since this disease. Now if the phone rings and she is at home, I don't even try to answer it because it is much easier for her to talk to people than it is for me. I had a stranger think that I have a mental disability because I could not talk well on the phone.

I can see that being left alone could be a serious problem if my spirits weren't high each day. If I wasn't busy that could certainly be the case. But because I spend quite a bit of time in devotions every day, the Lord helps to keep my spirits high. If I were prone to depression, it wouldn't be good for me to be left alone.

As it is, I don't suffer depression so I enjoy being alone very much. There are times of course, when I want to get out of the house just to join the outside world a little bit, but that only happens once or twice a week. After all, there isn't too much I can do outside of our home.

I am really happy that the Lord helps me each day. I do not know how I could cope every day without God's help in my life. Because He is always close to me I prefer to be alone because I can feel His presence near me when I am by myself. I love to be in His presence! There have been times in the past, where I have felt depressed, but that doesn't last very long. God is always there to help.

Feelings of Frustration and Depression

I was surprised when I looked through my memoirs and saw the number of times I felt frustrated or depressed. I wrote down my thoughts from August 6, 2004 until February 8, 2005, and during that time I wrote thirty-four typewritten pages. In those pages and over that time I had seventeen occasions where I wrote about frustrations or depression. That seems like quite a few, since I generally have a positive outlook on life. Here is what I wrote on a few days. On August 6, I wrote:

> My biggest frustrations come because of my speech and the actions of my mouth. Some mornings I awaken feeling quite low because it takes me such a long time to get to writing. Even eating breakfast takes so long, and grinding up my pill takes longer than just swallowing it. Eating generally takes much longer than normal, so I have to learn to eat less. God has really ministered to me at these times by having people phone me from

a long ways away. He has ways of encouraging me, and I feel grateful.[12]

You can see that even quite early in the process I was feeling frustrated over my speech and the problems with my mouth but notice how God was there to help me get over this problem! On August 8th I was depressed as well, but God again intervened:

> For some reason, I felt quite "down" today. At times I really feel like retreating from everything and everyone, and being by myself. Other times I wonder if my work is worth it. I have to persevere and do what I can to bring glory to God. Today, Trevor's sermon was good for me for it included an encouragement to keep fighting the good fight of faith.[13]

Our son Trevor was at that time pastor of a church here in Edmonton that we attend. Trevor has subsequently resigned from that church. At that time, God was again faithful in ministering to me through what Trevor had to say. Another occasion that I was depressed was on August 24:

> Today I woke up feeling quite depressed, but I decided to have devotions first of all. I was just tired of my situation. However, reading the scriptures and talking to God made me feel a lot better. Then as I exercised I was also feeling good.

You can see that again God came to my rescue when I was feeling depressed. He is always faithful! Also you can see the importance of me being able to exercise.

We have a treadmill that I was using. I walked for thirty minutes a day. Since we have moved, I have preferred to get outside to do some walking. In bad weather I could still use the treadmill, walking slower than I did before. With the way the disease is starting to affect my breathing, I have to guard against getting too tired because once my energy is gone I will be tired for the rest of the day.

I have been frustrated and embarrassed over the way my emotions have been acting out on me at times. This seemed to be exemplified after church one Sunday (recorded on October 5):

---

[12] "Thoughts Regarding a Fatal Disease," page 4

[13] ibid, page 4

I have a great deal of problems with regards to my emotions. I get embarrassed at times when I cannot speak properly because I'm shedding tears. I wish that wasn't the case, but I guess that it is part of my life until the Lord heals me or takes me home. Last Sunday was bad. I told my story of why I feel God has allowed this condition to come upon me a total of three times. The first time I told Russ (a friend) I was okay. When I repeated it to Ann and then to Trevor and Karen, I could hardly get it out because of my emotional outburst. This problem seems to be getting worse as the days go on, and that is a big concern for me. However, it seems that this too is something I have to learn to live with.[14]

This illustrates the kinds of concerns that I have been having as a result of the progression of this disease. As time has gone by, I think that I have gotten to the place where I can live with my condition. Possibly I am able to accept my condition as it has progressed. I am not quite as concerned as I was when it was developing, though I certainly have a greater concern with regards to my inability to speak. That probably is my biggest concern that I now face and have to be able to live with.

One day later on October 6, I had probably one of my worst days of depression:

This morning I had a period of time when I felt in despair for some reason. It happened right after I finished reading my ten chapters of scripture. After prayer, however, things started getting better. I think the despair came from the feeling that I was helpless in my situation, and that my life was always the same. I could not "get out and work" as I had done for my whole life. However, I have to remind myself that I can accomplish just as much at home.[15]

This again illustrates the feelings I went through when I realized that my life had to change completely. For a person who has worked hard for all of his life, it was hard to adjust to the fact that I could not continue working as I had been. Now my wife Ann is the primary bread-earner for our home and taking on this role has been very difficult for her at times. Before if things were not going well at work she really didn't have to work because I was bringing home a pretty good pay cheque.

---

[14] "Thoughts Regarding a Fatal Disease," page 17

[15] ibid, page 17

Now though, we depend upon her income for us. That changes things for her, and adds to the pressure I have because I can't get out and work like I used to.

On October 21st, I wrote this in my memoirs:

I have been thinking about my speech that is progressively going down hill. It is getting so bad that Ann cannot understand what I am saying at times. I am now thinking that it might not be too long before people will not understand what I am saying. I will have to be looking at alternate forms of communicating with people. When I consider that, it is quite depressing for me. It is going to be a hardship for me. I hope that I won't have to put up with that for very long. I need a healing touch, Lord! It makes me think that I won't be able to visit with people very much. Even now it has become a problem to order something in a restaurant because people have to ask me what I said. Hopefully I will be healed soon! [16]

Again you can see that with the changes going on with my speech, it has been a depressing time for me. At that time I was still eating regular food, but things have regressed, so restaurants are out of the question. I need a healing touch from the Lord! Meanwhile I guess I simply have to try to do the best with what I have.

Ann is also very helpful if I feel down in my spirit. I recorded an example of this on October 29th. I thank God for the faithful wife that He gave to me!

There was one evening when I had a particularly difficult time eating some food that should have been quite easy to eat (as it was a little while ago) that I ended up getting pretty depressed about things. However, Ann was really good for me. She got me playing a game on the computer and I got over the problem pretty soon. [17]

You can see that I have a pretty good support network, especially with my wife. She is usually strong when I have feelings of depression.

---

[16] "Thoughts Regarding a Fatal Disease," page 20

[17] ibid, page 22

I'm sure if you asked her she would say the same thing about me helping her. I certainly wish that I could help her more!

On November 3rd you can see how I felt when my condition was getting worse:

> I have been concerned about a few things in the last week or so. First of all, I have been coughing a lot more than usual. I sometimes cough when I am eating or drinking. That results with things flying out of my mouth all over the place. I have also had more problems with drinking recently. Water or juice often comes back out of my mouth. This can end up on the front of my shirt or it can go flying away. I have to remind myself to swallow the liquid when I am drinking it. This kind of action always makes me quite discouraged, particularly if I can't drink a glass of water without spewing it out a lot.[18]

Each major change that takes place in my body can potentially create some discouragement if I allow if to do so. I know that this is the devil's plan, and I definitely do not want to accept what he wants me to have. It is sometimes difficult to fight against discouragement when I can see what is happening to my body. God gives grace for me to handle each step in the journey, as long as I live close to Him. He is the One I really need to draw near to. But Ann and I have grown closer over the last year as well and I thank God for that.

There are other times when I felt frustrated, especially in January when my lungs didn't get cleaned out from my stay in the hospital in December. It was quite difficult to accept when I came down with a more severe form of pneumonia. I was concerned that this was going to be a monthly occurrence, because I knew that my body was not strong enough to develop a resistance. I do not want to die because of pneumonia!

I thank God that He has kept me out of the hospital now and that I have a respiratory therapist checking on my lungs each week. Also she has given me a nebulizer with a medication that becomes a mist that I can breathe into my lungs. This means that I will be more protected from lung infection, for which I praise God!

I have become adapted to getting my food through a tube so it looks like I will survive longer than I originally thought even if the Lord

---

[18] ibid, page 22

does not heal me. I also receive good care from the medical staff. However my time on earth depends on how fast the disease moves into my lungs.

In spite of the feelings of frustration and depression, I can confidently say that God has kept my spirit high. I am not dwelling on my problems, but simply trying to adapt to them. From a spiritual perspective, I can fly high over my problems and have victory. I will develop this more in a future chapter.

How Lack of Sleep has Affected Me

I am having trouble with sleeping. It could be because of this that my moods are quite often affected. This seems to be a problem with people living with bulbar ALS. Doctors have also thought I am having problems with getting enough oxygen as I sleep. So I decided to do some research in my memoirs to see if lack of sleep has been a consistent problem.

Often when you don't get a good sleep one night you will make up for it the next. With me, that hasn't always been the case. One day in a Doctor's office Ann reminded me how many times I had spoken of not getting a very good sleep. When I checked through my memoirs I found that there were seventeen occasions where I mentioned it.

This seems to be a greater problem as time goes by. There were three times in September, three times in October, five times in November, five times in December, and once in January. It could well be that in January I had so many other things happening with the ten days in the hospital that I didn't consider it as an important item to record.

I took myself off sleep medication about three years ago, and have usually been able to sleep well - until this disease caught up with me. Allow me to share some of my journey through this problem.

I wrote this on November 19th:

I guess I will have to start taking medication at night so that I can get a better sleep. My sleep has been inconsistent this week, and last night was particularly bad. I don't know if that is a trademark of this condition or not. I don't think I am under a lot of stress, but I am having trouble sleeping. When I have problems like these, I automatically awaken around 6:00 A.M. because that is the time I have awakened for many years. I really feel it, however, when I cannot get to sleep shortly after I go to bed at night.[19]

Not being able to get to sleep as soon as I go to bed has been a problem for a long time and continues to be. These days (April) I wake up around 5:00 A.M. and sleeping little after that.

On November 29th, I wrote more about another problem that I have with sleeping:

> When I lie down to go to sleep at night, it doesn't seem to matter how tired I am – it still takes me some time to settle down. I don't know if this is related to the disease or not. Usually I get a good sleep and only about once or twice a week I don't – on those nights I am awake for a while. If I wake up at five o'clock in the morning, I mostly likely don't get back to sleep. This morning I dosed until about 8:00 A.M., which was pretty good for me.[20]

This is about what my present sleep pattern is like (April, 2005). It takes time for me to get to sleep - last night I was in bed for one hour. Even when I get to sleep later, I still wake up at about 5:00 A.M. and doze off and on until I need to have my breakfast tube feeding.

December 9th and December 10th provide more examples of what has happened when I should be asleep.

> Last night I did not sleep very well for the second night in a row. However, I do not feel too tired. Last night was the first time that my nose was plugged even with the nasal strip on. It cleared up, but it kept me awake. I also had a weird thing happen with my mouth. I was awake when this happened. My mouth in front of my teeth and behind my upper lip suddenly became parched and dry. Inside my teeth, everything was okay (as much as it can be!). I had to lie on my stomach and with my finger-spread saliva on the inside of my lip to get it moistened up. It was weird, but I guess it goes with the condition.[21]

---

[19] "Thoughts Regarding a Fatal Disease," page 25

[20] "Thoughts Regarding a Fatal Disease", page 26

[21] ibid, page 28

Last night I slept well for half a night and not so well for the rest of the night. I felt quite tired this morning, but I have been busy doing things so I am not feeling too bad. My mouth is the usual challenge but all I need to do is adapt to the changes and keep my spirit up.[22]

My left nostril being plugged up has caused me some problems with sleeping. The nasal strip usually helps but there can be nights where I cannot breathe through my nose. Sometimes it is better for me to sleep with my mouth open because I can breath and my saliva can dry up almost completely.

I have recently (April, 2005) taken to lying on my back when I first go to bed so that the saliva problems can the cleared up soon. However, before I go to sleep I end up turning over several times. For many years I slept on my stomach, but since I have the tube I cannot lay that way. So sleeping on my side has become an adjustment.

There were a few occasions where I had a good sleep but still felt tired in the mornings. This made the therapists and doctors think that I was not getting enough oxygen into my body or not able to expel carbon dioxide as I should. Here are notes on that written on December 7th and 8th.

I have slept very well for the last three days, but I still have a tendency to be tired. It could be because I haven't been doing too much recently. I haven't been able to write much in my book for the last few days.

I feel better today as far as my spirit is concerned. Yesterday, though I had a good sleep, I did not feel well emotionally. Today I am feeling much better, even though I didn't sleep as well last night. I guess I should be feeling very positive each day because I know that the Lord is with me. That is all that is important for me. I also got things accomplished yesterday, which is very important for me. I am hoping that I can do more of the same today.[23]

---

[22] ibid, page 28

[23] "Thoughts Regarding a Fatal Disease," page 27

Feelings of Being Trapped Within a Deteriorating Body

There are times when I get quite discouraged because of the way my mouth feels. I realize that my body is deteriorating quite quickly, and this is frustrating. I would rather be healed than being trapped in this body. Sometimes I feel that I would like to be free from my body in the way that it is today. My spirit is strong and usually unaffected by my condition, and still the desire to leave this body is powerful.

I suppose I feel as Job felt. Satan did everything he could to make Job turn against God, and he is doing the same thing for me. I know that God is all-powerful and that He could very easily heal my body. I just get tired of the deterioration, and I would like to be free of this body one way or another.

I feel less than human at times, because I cannot do what I have been able to do my entire life. I am not a normal human being because of what I have to do to stay alive. The tube in my stomach obviously will extend my life and that on one level is a good thing. But when I'm miserable, I recognize it simply extends the time that I have to walk through the valley.

I am in the Lord's hands and His ways are much higher than mine. He knows what is the best for me, otherwise He would have healed me already. I don't know what to do except to put up with the problems and continue the walking.

I like to eat something once in awhile, and apparently I can do that. However a little snack does not replace a good meal that I would appreciate more. Though a voice synthesizer is a big help it does not compare to my own ability to speak.

As time has past however, until October of 2005, I can no longer eat anything nor do I want to. I can take very little food into my stomach because a good part of it stays in my mouth. I usually have to clear it out with my finger or with my toothbrush. This developed over time!

I look forward to the day this body will be left behind, and I will be given an "immortal body." There is a wonderful passage of scripture that speaks of this:

> *When the perishable has been clothed with the imperishable, and the mortal with immortality, then the saying that is written will come true: "Death has been swallowed up in victory." Where, O death, is your victory? Where, O death, is your sting?* (1 Cor. 15:54, 55)

The entire 15th chapter of 1 Corinthians is a treasure to read because it speaks of the fact that the mortal, fleshly body cannot enter into heaven and tells how our mortal bodies will become immortal. Because I know this is true I am sincerely longing to get rid of this body. If God chose to heal me entirely that would be okay, because then I could live on this earth about twenty more years unless the Lord returns soon – more of this in a later chapter! This disease has made me more conscious of how much I would like to be changed, and free of my present body.

I am sure that many others who have a similar condition in their body would have like feelings. I would be remiss not to point out that mortal is changed to immortal only if you have accepted Christ as your Saviour. I hope these thoughts that I have shared with you demonstrate the need I have to rely on the Lord for everything. My body is unable to do the things I have always done, so I need the Lord to help me in everything that I do.

In the next chapter I will discuss more about how God has been so precious as I have walked through the valley. I have been learning that I must depend upon the Lord for all that I do. I cannot hold it as an idea in my head or a sentiment in my heart. I need Him, and I would truly be a fool if I didn't realize that.

Chapter Eight:

Leaning on the Lord

In the time it has taken to write this book, bulbar A.L.S. is not standing still. My condition is changing. It is going downhill and it is progressing very quickly. My latest concern has been whether or not the disease is moving downward into my lungs. I found out about that yesterday.

An Update on My Condition

Yesterday (April 7th) we attended a clinic for A.L.S. patients and found a biPap machine was highly recommended by the specialist. This is to ensure that I get enough oxygen and get rid of carbon dioxide when I am sleeping. The last blood test showed my oxygen count as normal and so I thought that I would not need a biPap machine. However, there were other pulmonary tests that indicated that I am not doing too well with my breathing.

In the test taken in October, my ability to draw in air was very good, as well as my ability to expel my carbon dioxide. There is a scale from 1% to 100% to rate the ability to expel carbon dioxide. In October my score was over 100%. On the same Pulmonary Test performed in March, my score was 79%. My ability to expel carbon dioxide was reduced by at least 21%

On April 7th different tests were taken to see if what was done before was accurate. I was asked to take a deep breath in and then breathe out the best I could. In another phase of this test I was asked to cough as hard as I could. In this test there was a scale for adults where the normal was around 60 for breathing in and out. I was able to breathe in at a level of 30. I could expel only at 23. It showed the same as the previous test in that I have lost much of my ability to breathe normally.

This means that the disease is affecting muscles that are related to my diaphragm. I will need mechanical help to be able to breathe in air and to expel my carbon dioxide. So the biPap machine was introduced to my wife and me. A request is being put to our government to assist in paying for this relatively expensive machine. So I will have some sort of machine helping me breathe at night. Later it might mean that I will need such a machine during the day as well.

We received a biPap machine on loan for a few months. I used it the first time that night. I did not sleep too well for a couple of nights. As a result of my lack of sleep I became very tired during the day, so I really didn't know how much the machine was helping me. I stopped using it.

After reporting the problem to the respiratory therapist, I obtained a mask that covers my mouth as well as my nose. The first night with the new mask was very good. I got a decent sleep. I can see this has a potential to help me.

The biPap machine is connected up with a warm water humidifier that helps my mouth not get too dry. I was coughing again quite a bit, but when I started using the biPap machine, my coughing stopped. I am happy about the results, but rather shocked as well, for I did not realize that I could be coughing because of a lack of oxygen. I can even cough during the day. But thank God that after using the biPap and the right mask my coughing during the day has significantly diminished.

In order to get used to the biPap machine I will be in the Intensive Care Unit in the Misercordia Hospital over a night. With this disease I have now visited every major hospital in Edmonton - a total of six. But I have to try to get used to the system. I believe that with God's help, my breathing will become more normal than it has been. I thank God for supplying me with such good professionals who can help in such ways.

I am also getting some very new action for controlling my saliva. My body has become used to the medication and is producing more saliva again. Recently I went to the Cross Cancer Institute and got radiation applied to some important saliva glands. The idea is to get these glands closed up so that I will not have too much saliva. I will be extremely happy if saliva production is sufficiently minimized!

I went to the hospital five times this week in order to get the radiation treatments. So far, there have been some positive results, but not as good as I was hoping for. Everything is contingent upon how much fluid (i.e. water) I take into my body and this depends upon the number of medications I must take.

And now I return to this chapter that I trust will be a blessing to you. May all of us truly learn to lean on Jesus!

Leaning on Jesus

God is the only One who can heal me of this terminal disease. There is no doubt that I need Him now more than every before. I need to be able to trust Him in all that I do, and beloved, that is exactly what I do. God has given us many promises in His Word, and He is always faithful to His promises. There is an old chorus that some of you might be familiar with. It goes something like this:

Learning to lean, I'm learning to lean
I'm learning to lean on Jesus.
Finding more power than I've ever known,
I'm learning to lean on Jesus!

Even though I have served God for more than forty years, I am now realizing the need to lean on Him in a far greater way. He is the only hope that I have for healing. Doctors have very few ideas as to what causes this disease and researchers are far from a cure. The best that can be done is to manage the symptoms.

God is the only One who can heal, so I have to depend completely upon Him. I must learn to lean upon Him even more than I ever have before. I need His power in greater ways. I need unhindered access to the holy place where I can access His power. I need to realize His healing touch as soon as possible!

God has truly been good to us. I know that He has used me to pray for people and to see them healed. I have also grown in Him, learning that in me there is no good thing. As Paul said in Romans: *"I know that nothing good lives in me, that is, in my sinful nature. For I have the desire to do what is good, but I cannot carry it out."* (Romans 7:18)

As I have matured in Christ, I know I need to rely totally on Him, because I can do nothing pleasing to Him through my sinful nature. I need to lean on Him! I was thinking this way last November, as I wrote in my memoirs:

I have a good relationship with God, and I feel Him close to me at all times. That helps me when embarrassing things come up, such as me coughing food across the table. I do really need to lean on Him at all times.[24]

---

[24] "Thoughts Regarding a Fatal Disease," page 26

This has been on my mind for quite awhile, mainly because God is the only One who can heal me at this time. All medical doctors can do is to try to make me as comfortable as possible, and help me live as long as possible. However, it is God Who is in control of my life, so He is the One that I must lean upon.

Throughout the years I have been living close to our Lord. I have known His power. I have seen Him heal other people as well as myself. I have seen a bit of His power. I have read in the Bible several times that Jesus has raised people from the dead and those who followed Him did the same.

That is the place where I am at right now. I depend totally upon Him to heal me. His timing for healing me might be the thing I have to consider.

The Story of Lazarus Being Raised From the Dead

The story of Lazarus is very interesting when I am considering my own healing. Lazarus and his two sisters were friends of Jesus. In John 11, Lazarus was sick and his sisters sent a messenger to tell Jesus. As it turned out, Jesus delayed His coming to heal Lazarus, and it was so that God the Father and His Son would be glorified through it. He waited until Lazarus was dead and buried for four days before He arrived in Bethany. His purpose was to teach people to have faith in God.

In my situation, there is no way that I would expect Christ to raise me from the dead. However as I was meditating upon it, the point that became important to me was the reason why God was waiting to heal me. In the story of raising Lazarus from the grave, Jesus said to Martha, one of the sisters of Lazarus, *"Did I not tell you that if you believed, you would see the glory of God?"* (John 11:40). We can see that Jesus delayed in His coming so that the glory of God could be shown. In Jesus' prayer before he command Lazarus to come forth, He said He was doing this *"that they might believe that You sent Me."* (John 11:42)

All of this says to me that Jesus might be delaying healing me so that God could be glorified. I think that if He healed me even now, even those who don't know Him would certainly glorify him. Somehow His delay in healing seems to be tied to this. So I was wondering if eventually my healing might even mean the salvation of some people. I really do not know the answer to this, but I am sure that God does!

If He plans to heal me, I am sure that He wants several who know me but don't yet know Him to bring Him glory. On the other hand if He isn't planning to heal me, I hope the life that I am living now can still bring glory to Him!

Jesus said in that same chapter something that should be a great assurance to anyone who knows Him: *"Jesus said to her, 'I am the resurrection and the life. He who believes in Me will live, even though he dies; and whoever lives and believes in Me will never die. Do you believe this?'"* (John 11:25, 26)

This is one of the greatest promises that we have in the Word of God. Even if we die we will have eternal life. Jesus asked Martha whether or not she believed what He had said. The question that He asked Martha could be a question for each one of us. "Do you believe this?" I ask you if you believe that Christ is Who He said He is. This is vital for your own salvation.

I really don't think that anyone could doubt His power. I do know that in a flash He could heal me. His power is readily available to anyone who has faith to believe. Therefore does He delay because I am lacking in faith? Has Satan got some sort of power over me? Or is Christ simply delaying His healing touch because He wants to see His glory revealed? I know that if I was healed immediately, there would be many doctors and nurses who would really have to believe in His healing power. There would be no other recourse if I could be talking normally and be able to eat food easily. It would be pretty solid evidence that God heals, and His healing power is readily available to anyone who believes.

My Future Is Secure in Him

I am truly leaning on the Lord because I know that my future is secure in Him. If He has chosen to take me home, I know that I will see Him face to face. I know that my body will not be under the curse of this disease any longer. Rather, I will experience freedom from this mortal body and I will be clothed with a glorified body – something we can only dream about in this world.

That is why I don't fear death. The result of me dying of this disease simply opens the door to vast blessings for me. I am very confident of that happening. He is Lord of all!

Do *you* have the same assurance for your life that I have? I certainly hope so, because Christ has made a way for us to receive it.

Along with my future being secure I am very secure today. Both are because I am a servant of God. I have the faith to believe that He will not leave me with this disease. I feel that He is going to heal my body so that I can serve Him more effectively in the years to come. I know that He will be with me no matter what He decides to do with me. With God there is no way for me to lose.

Christ's Role in Creation

He is the Creator of this world and this universe. We read about Christ's role in creation from the following verses:

> *In the beginning was the Word, and the Word was with God, and the Word was God. He was with God in the beginning. Through Him all things were made; without Him nothing was made that has been made. In Him was life, and that life was the light of men. The light shines in the darkness, but the darkness has not understood it.* (John 1:1 - 5)

We find here that Christ was involved in creating the entire world. The entire Trinity (Father, Son, and Holy Spirit) was all involved in the creation of the world. As the Creator of the world, our God also created every person who is living in this world. He is the One who controls how long we live, and He is the One who loves each one with an everlasting love. Consequently God knows more about us than we know about ourselves.

Scripture says those who don't know Christ as Lord and Saviour are living in darkness. That is why they cannot understand the salvation and the healing that He offers to everyone.

Because God is our Creator, He knows more about us and more about the disease that I have than anyone else, including those who specialize in A.L.S. He knows how I can be healed better than anyone else does. He knows which cells have been put to death in my brain stem, and He alone has the power to bring them back to life. That is why I have the fullest confidence in Him, and that is also the reason why I need to lean on Him. He is the greatest security that can be found in this world, and I give Him praise for that!

A Look At What God Thinks of Our Life Span

Because God is my Creator and my Saviour, He also knows what is best for me. After all, He is also eternal. The life that we live on this earth is very short - even if we live a hundred years. One hundred years is a very short time when we think about eternity. Here is how the Bible declares a person's life span in this world:

> *As for man, his days are like grass, he flourishes like a flower of the field; the wind blows over it and it is gone, and its place remembers it no more. But from everlasting to everlasting the LORD'S love is with those who fear Him, and His righteousness with their children's children - with those who keep His covenant and remember to obey His precepts.* (Psalm 103: 15 – 18)

> *All men are like grass, and all their glory is like the flowers of the field. The grass withers and the flowers fall, because the breath of the LORD blows on them. Surely the people are grass. The grass withers and the flowers fall, but the word of our God stands forever.* (Isaiah 40:6b – 8)

There are many other verses that point out the fact that our time on earth is very short and transitory. What is our lifetime like when you compare it with eternity?

A Short Discussion About Eternity

I wanted to give you some information about where you might spend eternity. It is not that I want to scare you in any way, but rather to inform you of the choices you have to make because of the eternal nature of your soul.

Please understand that our souls are eternal whether or not you believe in Jesus Christ as your Saviour. According to the Bible, if you to not know Christ as your Saviour you will spend an eternity *"in the darkness where there will be weeping and gnashing of teeth."* (Matthew 25:30) That will mean eternal torment for you. But if you are a believer, you have a much greater place to spend eternity – in God's presence in Heaven!

It is important to understand that we cannot judge whether or not someone has gone to Hell or to Heaven. Jesus Christ is the only One who will judge where a person spends eternity. The One who will judge the entire earth will judge rightly. We can find such material in the White Throne Judgment that is found in Revelation 20:

> *Then I saw a great white throne and Him who was seated on it. Earth and sky fled from His presence, and there was no place for them. And I saw the dead, great and small, standing before the throne, and books were opened. Another book was opened, which is the book of life. The dead were judged according to what they had done as recorded in the books. The sea gave up the*

dead that were in it, and death and Hades gave up the dead that were in them, and each person was judged according to what he had done. Then death and Hades were thrown into the lake of fire. The lake of fire is the second death. If anyone's name was not found written in the book of life, he was thrown into the lake of fire. (Revelation 20:11 – 15)

Please notice that the term "Hades" is synonymous with the term "Hell." Anyone who has been sent to Hell will eventually end up in the Lake of Fire where their souls will be under torment forever.

But thank God, that my name is recorded in the Book of Life, and my future is heaven. None of our imaginations can dream about what God has planned for us there. My future is very secure.

Is yours?

I hope so! If not, you still have time to accept Christ as your Saviour!

Because my future is secure, I know that I need the Lord more now than ever before! Therefore I am leaning on Him, allowing Him to guide me, and do whatever He wishes for me. I do expect that His will is to see me healed so that I can become an ambassador for Him in the years to come.

My Need for Close Communion with God

I have been telling you that I feel that I am very close to God. However, I know that I should get much closer to Him. When a follower of Christ walks through the everyday of life, he or she most likely does not take the time to study the Word or spend time in intercession and supplication. We all know we can do better.

I have been spending time with God, particularly when I served a church as pastor. Then I had to study the Word and be in prayer much more to do just to do what I needed to do.

Once a follower of Christ develops a disease, spending time with God can get more difficult - even though I have time to do that now.

I have been having devotions for one and a half hours each day, but recently I have been having problems staying awake. I was able to read the Bible through in seven months, but at times I struggled to concentrate on what God was saying through His Word. I have a tendency to fight sleepiness during that time.

This factor is related to my ability to get enough oxygen when I am reading. I get a lot more oxygen when I am going for a walk. As I walk I do deep breathing exercises, knowing that this is good for my lungs.

There are other factors, such as the radiation treatments. I was told that radiation makes a person tired, and I found that was true! For the first time I fell asleep while I was praying (April 12th). This is rather embarrassing for me, but I realize that other forces are at work. I am sure the enemy would want me to be over-tired!

I need to try to get enough sleep at night so that I won't be tired during the day. However, a person with this illness usually gets more and more tired toward the end of his life. I do not at this point feel that I am coming to the end of my life, but there are signs indicating that my lungs are getting weaker. I recently found out at the bottom of my right lung there are sections that do not take air into them. This could be a sign that the disease is spreading.

I hope you see what the message is here for everyone. While we are feeling well we need to take the time to seek after God, because when you are sick, though you then will have time, the conditions might be similar to mine: you won't be as effective in prayer as you could be now.

Now is the time to seek the Lord – not when you are sick and really need His help. There could be a time when He will not be found: *"Seek the LORD while He may be found; call on Him while He is near. Let the wicked forsake his way and the evil man his thoughts. Let him turn to the LORD, and He will have mercy on him, and to our God, for He will freely pardon."* (Isaiah 55:6, 7)

I am glad that my life has been one of seeking after the Lord. However, now I must seek Him as I never have before. It is a struggle for me, but I have a desire to see God face to face, and be able to discuss this disease with Him. No one can look at God's face and live, but God could send an angel to tell me what my future is going to be.

I feel God's presence is very close to me at all times. His presence is very dear to me, because I can speak to Him at any time when I need His help. Still I am thirsting for more of God, and I can't be fully satisfied if I keep falling asleep while in prayer!

You can see that this is a real struggle for me. I am hungry for more of God, and I want to hear from Him in a definite way, but I am limited because of factors associated with my condition. Healing could come to me if I just demonstrated that I have faith in Him and His power to heal.

I do have faith that He is going to heal me, but what I really want is to get to know Him better. This disease has given me a greater hunger for Him than I have ever had, but the frustration of it is that I have not been able to pursue Him, as I desire.

There is an important verse of scripture. It is about seeking after God. *"Sow for yourselves righteousness, reap the fruit of unfailing love, and break up your unplowed ground; for it is time to seek the LORD, until He comes and showers righteousness on you."* (Hosea 10:12)

This speaks of the farmer and his responsibilities, but on the spiritual level it applies to all of us. We need to break up the ground of our heart that has hardened and has certain weeds in it – weeds such as self-righteousness, pride, and the desire for pleasure.

As we seek the Lord we become aware of these things that separate us from Him so we can repent of such attitudes. As we do this, He will rain His righteousness upon us. He will reveal more of Himself to us each day.

Certainly those who are Christians have His righteousness on them now. However, we have conditions that keep us from truly seeking the Lord, even though the time to seek Him is now! We need to seek the Lord so that He reveals our shortcomings to us, and helps us to get rid of our sins.

I need to have a closer communion with Him than I have at the present time. His ways are higher than our ways, and I would like to get to know His ways more perfectly. God is good, and He is a great God for us to serve. Please pray for me if I am still around when you read this book, that I truly might be able to seek Him in a fuller way.

Leaning on the Lord Regardless of Our Physical Health

The chorus that I began this chapter with has the line in it: "I'm learning to lean on Jesus." This is a lifetime experience for us. We have to make Him Lord of our lives if we really want to lean upon Him.

The problem lies with the fact that when we are feeling good, and are free from any disease, we think that we can do everything using our own strength. It is an attitude that is not different from what non-Christians might have. It is unfortunate that God has to give us difficulties for us to come to the place where we are depending on Him to meet every need.

I am afraid that many people in the Church are not that serious about making Christ Lord of their lives. It is my hope that you are not one of them. For it is only when we truly give Him everything that we can lean on Him and expect Him to help us in every situation. He needs to be Lord of all.

The Apostle Paul had similar views in regards to our dedication to God. He wrote:

> *Therefore, I urge you, brothers, in view of God's mercy, to offer your bodies as living sacrifices, holy and pleasing to God—this is your spiritual act of worship. Do not conform any longer to the pattern of this world, but be transformed by the renewing of your mind. Then you will be able to test and approve what God's will is—His good, pleasing and perfect will.*
> (Romans 12:1, 2)

I echo Paul, and urge everyone to offer your body to Him as a living sacrifice. Jesus died for our sins, so it is only natural that we should yield our bodies to Him. We no longer live the way we have in the past, but we allow ourselves to be transformed into a disciple of Christ by having our minds renewed by the Holy Spirit. Our lives are indeed changed when we accept Christ into our life. But our lives also continue to change as we continue to walk in our Christian life, allowing the Holy Spirit to work in our hearts and minds.

The apostle Paul had more to say about how we should live our Christian lives:

> *Be imitators of God, therefore, as dearly loved children and live a life of love, just as Christ loved us and gave Himself up for us as a fragrant offering and sacrifice to God. But among you there must not be even a hint of sexual immorality, or of any kind of impurity, or of greed, because these are improper for God's holy people. Nor should there be obscenity, foolish talk or coarse joking, which are out of place, but rather thanksgiving. For of this you can be sure: No immoral, impure or greedy person—such a man is an idolater—has any inheritance in the kingdom of Christ and of God.*
> (Eph 5:1 – 5)

We truly are to be imitators of God, showing God's love to everyone around us. When we do the sort of things that are talked about in this passage, we are no different from the world. We cannot inherit the kingdom of God if we continue to live in such a way. God expects us to be transformed into His image, and not to be partaking of things that He would not want us to do.

I trust that what I have written in this chapter will awaken both Christians and non-Christians to the need for us to give everything we have to God, and to lean upon Him for the help we need.

I have no option but to lean upon Him totally. He is the One who can comfort me, strengthen me, and give me peace within my heart. This is a daily project with me, because factors enter into my life almost on a daily basis that I need to rely upon Him for. I am thankful to God that He has been very faithful to me and has met all my needs. I am still expecting Him to heal me as well!

In the next chapter I will focus on the victory that He gives to me in spite of my condition. God is very close to me, and I praise Him very much because of that. He is always there to help us in every situation.

Chapter Nine:

Living in Spiritual Victory

A very important aspect of living with Bulbar A.L.S. is the fact that I can have victory over the way my physical body is working by keeping my spirit strong through the help of God. There is absolutely no way that I could be at a place of victory if it wasn't for the help that the Lord has provided for me. It is true that there have been times of depression. But in total I can freely say that my feelings have been mostly positive, because I have learned to draw on God for help.

My Experience at Pastor's Camp and Subsequent Days

Before I went to Pastor's Camp last August (August 10th – 14th, 2004), I had been feeling under quite a bit of oppression. We had not yet received the doctor's official diagnosis but we were pretty positive that the sickness was bulbar palsy. We had not linked it to A.L.S., but as we researched, the possibility became clearer.

There was an overriding amount of oppression upon me that I finally realized at Camp. I began to understand during the service that the devil had put this on me. I recorded my experience in my memoirs:

> We attended Pastor's Camp and had a very good time. During the Wednesday service, I felt a real answer to some of the problems I had been having. I had felt quite depressed at times, particularly when it came time for me to start working on the book. I realized this was a satanic oppression, and told Ann about it after the service. She had O.J. and Barb {good pastoral friends of ours} pray for me (others joined in). That prayer broke the oppression that I was feeling. I also decided that I had to make some changes to be able the fight against the tactics of the enemy. I needed to pray more, and have a closer relationship with God.[25]

---

[25] "Thoughts Regarding a Fatal Disease," page 4

From that time on, I felt that a weight was taken off my shoulders. Then I was much freer to function in a victorious manner. It would be important for me to draw closer to God and to live close to Him at all times if I was going to continue to live in a victorious manner.

In the days that followed Camp, I made the changes that I thought would be necessary to be close to God. Victory over body ailments is important, because I want to be a good testimony for Christ at all times. Also, I do not want my wife and family thinking of me as a great complainer. It is easy to not complain about my condition when I have such support from the great God that we serve.

On August 16th, the same day that we obtained the official prognosis from Dr. Siddiqi, I began to make changes in my devotions. I recorded what I did in my memoirs:

> Today I started some new things. I increased my devotions from one hour to an hour and a half, mostly to be in the Word more. I also am going to praise God more in my prayer time. I feel it is imperative for me to feel God's presence with me in a greater way. [26]

At that time it worked quite well, and I had a good sense of communicating with God. His presence has always been very dear to me. While I still spend as much time, I now have more problems in trying to stay awake and absorbing what God wants to say to me. It is my hope that a longer sleep will help me out more. But I still have a good communion with God because I can talk to Him at any time of the day. I talk to Him when I am sitting down, and when I am laying in bed at night. He is always close to me.

On August 18th I recorded the result of increasing my devotions.

> I had my extended devotions and had a good time with God. I feel that I always have to sense victory in my spirit regardless of how my body feels, so that I can truly be "on top" and not depressed. I also exercised and had a good time with God during that time. On the one hand, it would be glorious for me to go home to be with Him. However, if He thinks I could be useful on earth, I would like to remain. I do want Ann to be well looked after. [27]

---

[26] "Thoughts Regarding a Fatal Disease," page 6

[27] ibid, page 6

My reference to being "on top" in this quotation comes from a popular passage in the Bible. This type of thinking must be applied to living a positive lifestyle, whether you have a fatal disease or not. Too many Christians are negative in their approach to life. This takes a good testimony for God away from them.

> *The LORD will make you the head, not the tail. If you pay attention to the commands of the LORD your God that I give you this day and carefully follow them, you will always be at the top, never at the bottom. Do not turn aside from any of the commands I give you today, to the right or to the left, following other gods and serving them.* (Deuteronomy 28: 13, 14)

God was giving His people very important instructions about how to live. He wants us to be the "head" and not the "tail" as well as "at the top" and "never at the bottom." He says that we can be in that place if we carefully follow what the scriptures tell us to do. We must not be following other gods, which became the demise of the Israelites.

Following other gods does not necessarily refer to the gods of the dim and distant past. People today are also serving gods – gods of entertainment, including sports and other forms; and gods of power and prosperity. People do a lot to try to become rich, including spending substantial amounts of money on gambling and lotteries. May we look to the God of the Bible, Who gives us clear instructions about how to live.

I can always be "on top" because my spirit is not affected by the problems that my body is going through. Our God is a God of great power and He will help us always to have victory in our spirits. If I follow the scriptures as I should, I will never be underneath, but rather on top in every situation.

It doesn't matter whether I go home to be with Him or stay here and minister to Him on a regular basis. From my viewpoint it is up to God to exercise His will in my life. I belong to Him completely and if I remain on earth I will continue to be used by Him. If I go home to be with Him, that would be my greatest blessing for sure. However, it is all up to Him. I believe that He will heal me, but if He doesn't, that is okay as well.

There is one more quote from my memoirs that I want to share with you, because God was helping me to a great extent. Also I found that getting exercise is something that brings encouragement. I wrote this on August 29th:

I am feeling pretty good today. I spent an hour and a half in devotions and exercised for half an hour as I usually do. I prayed for my family as well. I want God to really speak to their hearts. My speech has not improved much yet, and I still bite my lips or cheeks at times. However, I have found that I can have victory in spite of those problems.

I have been thinking about what it would be like if I didn't have Christ as my Saviour and Helper. It certainly would be a different story than it is now! God is my strength, and I lean on Him every day. Think of it – if I die, like Paul it would be a better place for me to be than it is now. However, it would be hard on Ann and the family. Therefore it is up to God to heal me.[28]

You can see how God has been working in my life right from the start, before my condition advanced to where it is now (May 25, 2005). He is giving me freedom from how my body feels and a sense of victory in my spirit. I thank God for His help that He has given to me. It is important to be able to communicate with my God on a regular basis, and now I find that I can be talking to Him at different times throughout the day. He is always there to listen. I am also careful to praise Him for the victories that He brings. Though the situation with my body can be very difficult at times, I can still have a good time in my spirit, because God is with me.

Living in Victory Though My Body is Physically Losing Strength

Since my last visit to the hospital, I find that I don't have the strength in my body the way that I used to. Now jobs that once were very easy are now much more difficult. I could not help too much with our move to our new home.

When people look at me they say that I am looking pretty good, but being robbed of my strength has caused me to change my physical actions. I cannot take part in the things that I used to, especially if they are physical in nature. It doesn't mean that I don't want to help, it's that if I work too hard one day I will be totally washed out the next. My strength does not come back to me the way that it should. Now I can get

---

[28] "Thoughts Regarding a Fatal Disease," page 9

pretty tired out just carrying something up the stairs or carrying things that I didn't consider heavy at one time.

But God has some plans for me - and for everyone who is going through a similar walk. Paul wrote some words that explain what I have been saying:

Therefore we do not lose heart. Though outwardly we are wasting away, yet inwardly we are being renewed day by day. For our light and momentary troubles are achieving for us an eternal glory that far outweighs them all. So we fix our eyes not on what is seen, but on what is unseen. For what is seen is temporary, but what is unseen is eternal. (2 Corinthians 4:16 – 18)

It is important for us to be renewed in God every day, so our focus is not on what is temporary, but rather what is eternal. The troubles that we have on this earth cannot be compared with the glory we will know in the future. This is a great hope that each believer should have, but I wonder how many who claim to be Christians actually have this feeling in their hearts. We need to be focused heavenward!

It should be our focus whether we are sick or not. God wants to take us to that place in the Spirit where we catch a glimpse of what He has planned for each one who wants to live forever. Simply reading His Word will help you to realize what our focus should be in this life.

Paul wrote another passage that relates to the last one. He gives us an idea of where our viewpoint should come from. May we deliberately change our focus from this earth to the things of God.

Since, then, you have been raised with Christ, set your hearts on things above, where Christ is seated at the right hand of God. Set your minds on things above, not on earthly things. For you died, and your life is now hidden with Christ in God. When Christ, who is your life, appears, then you also will appear with Him in glory. (Colossians 3: 1 – 4)

Our focus needs to be from above, not from on this earth. The death spoken of here is not physical death, but dying to the flesh, which God wants all of us to do. With our lives hidden in God, we can have victory in spite of what happens to our body.

Accepting Christ as Saviour and giving Him control of your life leads you into a relationship that is tremendous compared to that which the person without Christ might have. Our minds can be facing upwards at all times. Our focus can be on God, Who is eternal, rather than on this earth, which is temporary. God help us to keep our focus where it should be on a daily basis!

How a Strong Faith Frees Us from the Burden with Our Body

It is very obvious that we cannot completely ignore what is going on in our body. After all, we are physical as well as spiritual. However, if we live from the pretence that the physical is the most important, we would have to negate the importance of our God, because He is not physical.

At one time, Christ our Lord was a man, but His focus was one thing: it was always heavenward. He knew that His greatest function was to die upon the Cross so we could be free from our sins. From the thirty-three years (approximately) that He spent on earth, He opened up the doors of eternity so that we can be with Him forever.

Our focus therefore should not be on the physical but rather on the spiritual. "*He has made everything beautiful in its time. He has also set eternity in the hearts of men; yet they cannot fathom what God has done from beginning to end.*" (Ecclesiastes 3: 11) God has placed the thought of eternity in every person's heart, whether we have accepted Him or not. Today you can go to the most primitive tribe on earth and find that they have some form of religion because God has placed eternity in their hearts. But many have not understood that eternity is within their hearts, because their focus has been upon the transitory and not upon the eternal.

Faith is important in order to see our God. In fact, we cannot come to know Him unless we exercise faith. Again the Bible tells us that every person has been given a measure of faith. "*For through the grace given to me I say to everyone among you not to think more highly of himself than he ought to think; but to think so as to have sound judgment, as God has allotted to each a measure of faith.*" (Romans 12:3 NASB) Anyone who has lived on earth does have a measure of faith, whether you want to acknowledge it or not. It is interesting how God has made us, isn't it?

What is faith? How does faith helps us to live above the situation that our body is in?

We have the definition of faith in the following verse: "*Now faith is the assurance of things hoped for, the conviction of things not seen.*" (Hebrews 11:1 NASB) In other words, faith doesn't deal with the things that we can see with our naked eye. Rather, it has to do with the things that we cannot see.

We can see a lot with our spiritual eyes that we cannot with our physical eyes. Faith and hope are partners in the spiritual realm. Faith brings a conviction with it. We are certain that what we believe will come to pass. In the same way, I have the conviction that God will heal me.

God expects us to have faith. In fact, we have no place in His kingdom unless we exercise faith. *"And without faith it is impossible to please God, because anyone who comes to Him must believe that He exists and that He rewards those who earnestly seek Him."* (Hebrews 11:6) Faith is indispensable in order to please God. We also must believe that He will reward us if we seek Him. In my circumstances I must apply faith to every area of my life, believing that as I exercise faith and seek Him in an earnest way that He will reward me. That is my prayer and my desire and will continue to be so until God tells me something different.

Faith actually can separate us from our physical body because we are to walk by faith in everything that we do. *"We live by faith, not by sight."* (2 Corinthians 5:7) This means that we are not to place our focus on the physical, but upon that which is unseen.

I cannot ignore my physical body, because the frustrations of it are with me all of the time. However, I cannot live a victorious life if my sole focus is on the physical. In order to live in a victorious manner, I must look beyond this quickly regressing body, and look to the God Who has all power and all authority. I must keep my focus on the future where I will be totally free from this body, and have the certainty of one day having an immortal body in its place.

Speaking by faith, I know that a blessed future awaits me. I also feel that the day is coming soon when I can rejoice with all those who are praying for me that all their prayers have been answered. I will no longer have any trace of the disease in my body! Praise God for the victory that He gives!

Paul speaks about the victory that each Christian has in Jesus Christ. 1 Corinthians 15 is about the resurrection of Christ and the changes in our bodies that transform us from being mortal to being immortal. It will be a great time for us when Christ appears in the clouds! The last part of that chapter resounds with the victory that is ours through Jesus Christ.

> *I declare to you, brothers, that flesh and blood cannot inherit the kingdom of God, nor does the perishable inherit the imperishable. Listen, I tell you a mystery: We will not all sleep, but we will all be changed– in a flash, in the twinkling of an eye, at the last trumpet. For the trumpet will sound, the dead will be raised imperishable, and we will be changed. For the perishable must*

clothe itself with the imperishable, and the mortal with immortality. When the perishable has been clothed with the imperishable, and the mortal with immortality, then the saying that is written will come true: "Death has been swallowed up in victory. Where, O death, is your victory? Where, O death, is your sting?" The sting of death is sin, and the power of sin is the law. But thanks be to God! He gives us the victory through our Lord Jesus Christ.
(I Corinthians 15:50 – 57)

This then, is the victory for everyone who has the faith to believe what God has planned for us. There is a day coming when all believers who are alive will be taken up to heaven with bodies that have been transformed to glorious bodies rather than the ones we have now. I will be writing more about this in a later chapter, but please understand that death does not have victory over us!

Can you see why I have absolutely no fear of death? If you do not have faith in Christ, then you will have a fear of death that cannot be broken. Believe the good news of Jesus Christ! You do not need to fear death.

When I speak of having victory over the valley I am walking through with my body, that the victory is based upon the Word of God. It is not founded on some odd whim or fancy. It is, beloved, based upon fact!

I thank God for the victory that He gives. Each believer should rejoice because of the victory that is ours through Jesus Christ. We are not slaves to our mortal bodies, but rather our victory comes when we are transformed into imperishable (eternal) bodies.

Knowing the Peace That Transcends All Understanding

Having God's peace in our hearts regardless of what is happening with our bodies is another way of claiming the victory that God has given to us. Peace goes a bit farther than actually claiming victory over the affliction. Sometimes we can be quick to claim victory but we don't really have God's peace within our hearts.

I can safely say that as I have been walking close with God, He has given this sweet peace to both my wife and I. I am truly thankful that Ann knows this peace as well!

God's peace is something that comes when the world seems to be crashing in all around you. That is why Paul called it something we cannot really understand. *"And the peace of God, which transcends all understanding, will guard your hearts and your minds in Christ Jesus."* (Philippians 4:7) Notice what peace does for us – it guards our hearts and our minds. This is important because fear comes to both our hearts and our minds - if the devil has his way. This is truly a blessing of God which we cannot manufacture on our own. We need God's presence with us at all times so that His peace can guard our lives.

Jesus told us how we are to get this peace. It comes directly from Him! This is what Jesus said regarding this peace: *"Peace I leave with you; My peace I give you. I do not give to you as the world gives. Do not let your hearts be troubled and do not be afraid."* (John 14:27) Notice that Jesus gives us this supernatural peace. Because He gives us this peace, we are not to be troubled or afraid.

What happens if we **are** troubled and afraid? It means that we won't have peace. You see, before we can have this peace, we must exercise our faith in God. Being troubled or having fear is the opposite of having faith that God is with you and that He will help you. While we have a responsibility to have faith in God and in what He will do for us, He will grant us this supernatural peace – a peace that cannot be understood by those who don't know God. Thank God today for His peace!

Drawing Strength from God on a Daily Basis

In this situation, I need to gain strength from God on a regular basis. There is no other way for me to gain strength. Without gaining strength on a daily basis, I would have no sense of victory. My focus would then be turned to my physical body, which has become much weaker.

It is difficult for my body to gain more strength. Once I lose my strength, it takes a long time to recover. For this reason I constantly am depending upon God to give me strength on a daily basis. He has been very true to His Word in this area.

The Word of God is very important in that it tells us where our strength will come from. It comes directly from God as we seek Him.

He gives strength to the weary, and to him who lacks might He increases power. Though youths grow weary and tired, and vigorous young men stumble badly, yet those who wait for the LORD will gain new strength; they will mount up with wings like eagles, they will run and not get tired, they will walk and not become weary. (Isaiah 40: 29 – 31 NASB)

God looks after His people, though they might be extremely weak as I am today. As we wait upon the Lord for that strength, He gives strength to us. While our bodies might be failing us, our spirits will gain strength so that (in the spiritual realm) we can mount up with wings as eagles, flying above our problems at a level of spiritual victory.

It means waiting upon the Lord, and sometimes we are not seeking the Lord's help as much as we should.

There is another verse that Isaiah wrote which means a great deal to me. *"So do not fear, for I am with you; do not be dismayed, for I am your God. I will strengthen you and help you; I will uphold you with my righteous right hand."* (Isaiah 41:10) This shows that God is always close to us. Having fear, by the way, is the opposite of having faith. If we truly have faith, then there is no room for fear. Fear is the greatest tool that Satan has to use against us today. Understand that God is always with us to help us in any situation that we face. He is upholding me a great deal in these days as I face this disease.

We also see in Psalms another promise that means a great deal to me. *"God is our refuge and strength, an ever-present help in trouble."* (Psalm 46:1) It is the Lord who gives me strength each day. I need Him to be there to help, and He always is faithful. I am very thankful to God because He is there to give me strength whenever I need it. Believe me, there are times when my mouth feels terrible or when I have a cough every time I move. My body certainly isn't what it used to be, so I am thankful to God for keeping my spirit in victory.

In Paul's writings we can find several verses in which God gives strength to His people. A verse that is very significant to me is the following: *"But the Lord is faithful, and He will strengthen and protect you from the evil one."* (2 Thessalonians 3:3) Here we see that God will strengthen us and shelter us from the evil one, meaning the devil. The devil is behind this affliction. He might think he has gained the victory over me, but here we see that our God limits our enemy's plans. It is God who strengthens us, and it is God who protects us from the evil one. I am thankful to God that He is the One who is in control of my situation.

Whether I live or die, God will see to it that I am the winner. Death will become a victory or if I am healed (as I hope to be) that will be a victory. The only way that I can lose in this struggle is if I turn my back on God and say that He is not keeping His Word in my life.

How can I? I do not know what is best for me because my thoughts are very finite. God's plans for my life are infinite, so how could I complain? It is God who gives me the victory each day, and therefore I thank Him for that.

There may be some questions that some people have about being able to access God's strength in difficult situations. One of the greatest ways to gain God's strength is to be studying the Bible on a regular basis. The best avenue for me to gain strength is by concentrating on the promises of God - the Bible is full of them.

The Bible is like no other book you have ever read. As you read the scriptures, they come alive within your spirit. I don't know how many times I have read through the entire Bible, though in guessing how many times, I would say around twenty-five times at least. However, each time I read the Bible, God speaks to my heart in a new way. I especially like the prophets in this respect.

God, the Holy Spirit makes a certain passage important to you. The Bible is the only book that is inspired by the Holy Spirit. In the book of Hebrews we read this verse about the Holy Spirit working within our hearts: "*For the word of God is living and active. Sharper than any double-edged sword, it penetrates even to dividing soul and spirit, joints and marrow; it judges the thoughts and attitudes of the heart.*" (Hebrews 4:12) We see that the Holy Spirit is very active when we read God's word. The life within the Word of God is actually the Holy Spirit working within our hearts.

The only way that I can claim victory while in this deteriorating body is by gaining His strength day after day. He has been faithful to do that, so that I can truly live "above and not beneath." I praise Him for doing this for me.

The Need to Be Thankful in All Things

If we truly want to have God's blessing in our lives regardless of our physical condition, it is important that we have thankfulness in our hearts. Thankfulness to God shows that we are putting our trust in Him.

But, there are undoubtedly many who suffer from chronic diseases who have never felt that they should be giving thanks to God for it. I agree that this is difficult, but it is something that we should do.

In 1st Thessalonians, we find an important verse in regards to giving thanks: *"give thanks in all circumstances, for this is God's will for you in Christ Jesus,"*(1 Thessalonians 5:18).

It is clearly God's will for us to give thanks to Him in every circumstance (or disease) that we might find ourselves in. My question to fellow sufferers is this: do you give thanks to God each day, regardless how you feel?

Let me take this a step farther, so that we don't get lost in trying to defend ourselves for not being thankful to God while you are in bad circumstances. In the Letter to the Ephesians Paul writes about how we should be living this life.

> *Be very careful, then, how you live—not as unwise but as wise, making the most of every opportunity, because the days are evil. Therefore do not be foolish, but understand what the Lord's will is. Do not get drunk on wine, which leads to debauchery. Instead, be filled with the Spirit. Speak to one another with psalms, hymns and spiritual songs. Sing and make music in your heart to the Lord, always giving thanks to God the Father for everything, in the name of our Lord Jesus Christ.* (Ephesians 5:15 – 20)

I added a few verses so that all who read this book might see how God expects us to live these days. We need to know what the will of God is for our lives. We are living in the last days before Christ returns and we are not to act foolishly, doing things that go against what God has told us to do within His Word. We need to be filled with the Holy Spirit so that we will not want to do those kinds of activities.

The main reason for me sharing this passage with you is so that you can see how Paul (who wrote the passage from 1st Thessalonians as well) says we are to give thanks. We are to give thanks to God "for everything"! In other words, we are to give thanks to God for the incurable disease that we have, or the situation that we find ourselves in. This is harder to do than to thank God *in* every situation. How can we do that?

God's Word means exactly what it says. I am supposed to thank God for Bulbar A.L.S. At first glance that might seem ridiculous. But when you think about it, are we not supposed to trust God for every situation and problem? Remember that God is in control. He can at the snap of His fingers cure me of this disease if He so chooses.

But again we see that our ways are not His ways. He knows the end much better than we do, and He controls what happens in this world. So even though I have had questions for God concerning this disease, I do accept the fact that I have this disease, and I am thankful that He is the One in control, and He is the One who has prepared a place for me in heaven.

While it is difficult for me to be thankful for the way this disease is progressing throughout my body so quickly, I do give thanks for this disease. It has firstly given me time to write, and I believe that God has wanted me to be a writer for many years.

Secondly I am thankful for the ways that God has used me to be a blessing to others since I came down with this affliction. Several who have visited with us have gone away blessed because of the way my wife and I have handled this situation. If I can be a blessing to people in my death then that is great. If and when God heals me, this will be such a blessing to others that many might possibly come into God's kingdom. That would be a tremendous plus for me.

Thirdly, I am thankful to God for the great relationship that I have had with Ann. We have always had a good relationship, but our relationship has become dearer and more intimate than before. Ann has really gone out of her way to help me access the resources that are available. Our doctor friend told us that twenty years ago such resources never existed. Therefore we are extremely thankful to God for the medical resources that are available. We have come to know several professionals in the medical realm and have learned how they feel about their patients. That has been a real blessing for us.

Fourthly, I am thankful for the disease itself, because it has taught me to have a greater dependence upon God. This affliction cannot be cured by anyone in the medical profession, so I must depend upon God for everything including a complete healing. I depend upon Him for allowing me to get a good sleep at night, and I depend upon Him for giving Ann the strength that she needs on a daily basis. I depend on the food and other materials that I need to be delivered to our door, as I need them.

I truly have to be thankful to God for a variety of reasons. He has been a stronghold in this time of trouble! I realize that being thankful to God is important for our growth to spiritual maturity. What is truly means is that we are trusting God to be our help and our guide in every situation. May God help you to become thankful as well!

Chapter Ten:

The Future Glory All Believers Will Inherit

Why don't I have any fear about death? I know that one day all believers who die before Christ returns will inherit the glory God has in heaven. If we are still alive when Christ returns, we will see Him come and we will rise to meet Him with our bodies completely transformed.

We can all live in spiritual victory and we do so because of what Christ has prepared for us in heaven. The thought of going to heaven is a tremendous thrill for believers, so I want to share that with you now.

It is my hope that there will be some people reading this book who have not accepted Christ as your Saviour. I want to show you what you can look forward to in the future, though I will be centering on that in the next chapter.

For this chapter I want to focus on heaven, so you will be reminded or enlightened about living forever with Christ. Heaven is a wonderful place. I pray that everyone will be ready to celebrate Christ's coming back to this world, or possibly dying and going to heaven – in either event, being together with Jesus forever. Heaven is not for everyone, but it is for as many as who would receive.

Heaven – the Place Everyone Seeks After Death

Heaven is a wonderful place. It is a place that many people long for and expect to go when they die. Even many unbelievers feel that they will be going to heaven. Many believers feel that they will be going to heaven but they don't know what heaven will be like. Both groups are ignorant and need to be enlightened.

Randy Alcorn, who wrote a book called <u>Heaven</u> (published by Tyndale), stated in that book that many people feel in heaven there will be "nothing to do but float on clouds and strum harps." In reality, however, as he wrote, that we have "God to worship and serve; friends to enjoy; a universe to rule; and purposeful work to do."[29] We will have an exciting time to serve our God in heaven. The glories of heaven are

---

[29] From <u>Heaven</u> by Randy Alcorn, Eternal Perspective Ministries (http://www.epm.org)

so great that we cannot comprehend everything that is there because they are so much beyond our imagination.

When I think of heaven, I have a tendency to think of some hymns about heaven, because such hymn writers had glimpses of heaven we may have lost in our church culture. Here is one that concentrates on our emotions when we get to heaven. It is called "Heaven is a Wonderful Place!"

Heaven is a wonderful place, Filled with Glory and Grace,
I want to see my Saviour's face, Heaven is a wonderful place.

Hallelujah, 'Twill be Glory.
There'll be joy; there'll be music in the air.
There'll be singing; There'll be shouting,
When we all get together up there.

We can see that there will be a great deal of joy in heaven, and that joy will be ours for all eternity! We praise our God for that! I can hardly wait to go there because of God's marvellous presence and the love that will be shown there. He is truly a great God, but for all of us, in this life we cannot realize how great our God really is, for it is beyond our understanding. The Apostle Paul wrote of this: "*Now we see but a poor reflection as in a mirror; then we shall see face to face. Now I know in part; then I shall know fully, even as I am fully known.*" (I Corinthians 13:12) We truly will not know everything that is eternal in scope until our own bodies become immortal.

Another hymn writer composed a hymn called "How Beautiful Heaven Must Be." This speaks more about what the Bible says heaven will be like. I'll give you a few verses of this song that is very beautiful itself.

We read of a place that's called heaven
It's made for the pure and the free
These truths in God's Word He hath given
How beautiful heaven must be

In heaven no drooping nor pining
No wishing for elsewhere to be
God's light is forever there shining
How beautiful heaven must be

Pure waters of life there are flowing
And all who will drink will be free

Rare jewels of splendour are glowing
How beautiful heaven must be

The angels so sweetly are singing
Up there by the beautiful sea
Sweet chords from their gold harps are ringing
How beautiful heaven must be.

There are many other hymns about heaven that are wonderful to read the words of, and I encourage you to do so if you have a hymnbook at your disposal. The good hymns though, are hymns that a based upon the Word of God, because therein lies the truth about what heaven is truly like.

It my desire that everyone who reads this book will want to go to heaven. If I am to die before you do, I will be very happy to meet with you there. Heaven is truly a wonderful place to be! There will be all kinds of joy there for sure. The life that you are presently living might not have much joy in it but there is great potential for you to experience joy for eternity, free from the body that you possibly are suffering in.

That is the case for me. There are times when I feel that it would be great to be out of this mortal body that gives me so many problems. I am thankful though, to the God Who gives me strength for each day. Praise His name!

The Glorious Bodies Reserved For Believers

In the last chapter I wrote about the victory that is ours. When we rise to be with Christ at His coming, our bodies will be transformed from mortal to immortal bodies through the power of God (I Corinthians 15). That is the first step to be taken into God's glory for us. There are other passages that refer to this fact as well. It is known as the Rapture, which will take place during the first phase of Christ's second coming. Please notice what Paul wrote to those in Thessalonica:

Brothers, we do not want you to be ignorant about those who fall asleep, or to grieve like the rest of men, who have no hope. We believe that Jesus died and rose again and so we believe that God will bring with Jesus those who have fallen asleep in Him. According to the Lord's own word, we tell you that we who are still alive, who are left till the coming of the Lord, will certainly not precede those who have fallen asleep. For the Lord Himself will come down from heaven, with a loud command, with the voice of the archangel and with the trumpet call of God, and the dead in Christ will rise first. After that, we

who are still alive and are left will be caught up together with them in the clouds to meet the Lord in the air. And so we will be with the Lord forever. Therefore encourage each other with these words.
(1 Thessalonians 4:13 – 18)

This is a glorious passage written to assure Christians at the time that those who have died before Christ returned would still be resurrected at His coming. Those who die presumably won't have their glorified bodies until Jesus comes again with "those who have fallen asleep in Him." I assume that means the souls (and spirits) of those who have died in Christ will come back with Him when He comes and those who are already dead will be reunited with their bodies. We have another passage of scripture that amplifies this:

Therefore we are always confident and know that as long as we are at home in the body we are away from the Lord. We live by faith, not by sight. We are confident, I say, and would prefer to be away from the body and at home with the Lord. So we make it our goal to please him, whether we are at home in the body or away from it. (2 Corinthians 5: 6 – 9)

If we are at home in our body we are absent from the Lord, but if we are free from our bodies then we are present with the Lord, which Paul is saying that we prefer "to be away from our body and at home with the Lord." So when we die, our spirits leave our body and we are at home with the Lord. Then at the Rapture, we will be coming with Christ and our glorified body will become part of us. So death really means that our souls and our bodies are separated.

I remember seeing a program on television one time where scientists were studying whether or not a person lost weight when he died, or whether there were any changes. They had the person who was going to die on a scale. When he died, he didn't lose any weight but in a picture they saw a wisp of white going out of his body upwards.

We also have seen where people have died and have come back to life describing what they saw while being dead. Some spoke of being above their bodies, and seeing physicians working over their bodies. I think it is very true that once we die, we are freed from our mortal bodies and our spirits and souls, which are eternal, are what we have when we go home to be with the Lord. At the Rapture of the Church we are united with our gloried bodies that rise from the grave.

It will be a glorious time to be transformed into glorious bodies that are free from pain and disease. We have that explained to us in the following passage from Paul's writings: *"But our citizenship is in heaven. And we eagerly await a Saviour from there, the Lord Jesus Christ, Who, by the power that enables Him to bring everything under His control, will transform our lowly bodies so that they will be like His glorious body."* (Philippians 3:20, 21)

Our glorified bodies will be like Christ's resurrected body while He was on earth. We know that He reached a far greater level of glory when He ascended into heaven. But let's take a look at His resurrection body as we see it in scripture. I will share one passage with you, but there are others for you to look at. To set the stage for you, understand that His disciples were in a locked room discussing what they had heard about Jesus being resurrected:

> *While they were still talking about this, Jesus Himself stood among them and said to them, "Peace be with you." They were startled and frightened, thinking they saw a ghost. He said to them, "Why are you troubled, and why do doubts rise in your minds? Look at My hands and My feet. It is I Myself! Touch Me and see; a ghost does not have flesh and bones, as you see I have." When He had said this, He showed them His hands and feet. And while they still did not believe it because of joy and amazement, He asked them, "Do you have anything here to eat?" They gave Him a piece of broiled fish, and He took it and ate it in their presence.* (Luke 24: 36 – 42)

You can see many elements of His resurrected body. First of all, He could walk through walls. Secondly, His body was as flesh and bones. They could see the nail holes in His hands and feet. They also saw that He could eat as they did. That doesn't mean that He had to eat, because He didn't, but He wanted to show them He wasn't a ghost. By the way, we have pictures of His gloried body in Acts 9:3-9 and <u>Revelation 1:9-16</u> that I won't take the time to show to you. Notice however, the kinds of bodies we might have. Revelation shows us that we will be dressed in white robes. One thing we can say is that our immortal bodies will be very different than our mortal bodies. They will be free of all of the problems that we face today. Praise be to God!

We see from another passage that we will one day be like Christ. This is one that is written by the Apostle John: *"Dear friends, now we are children of God, and what we will be has not yet been made known. But we know that when He appears, we shall be like Him, for we shall see Him as He is."* (1 John 3:2) I cannot wait for the day when I see Christ face to face! It will be a glorious time for all Christians!

What Heaven Will Be Like

There are many aspects of heaven that we will not know about until we get there. But there are several scriptures that point out what heaven will be like. For example, Jesus said that He is preparing places for us. The following passage points that out:

Do not let your hearts be troubled. Trust in God; trust also in me. In my Father's house are many rooms; if it were not so, I would have told you. I am going there to prepare a place for you. And if I go and prepare a place for you, I will come back and take you to be with me that you also may be where I am. You know the way to the place where I am going. (John 14:1 – 4)

We know that those homes will be great places for us to live in. It will be different where we don't have to eat or sleep or any such thing. We will be spiritual beings and our focus will be upon our God. Jesus also said that in heaven there will be no marriages, and tells us what we will be like. *"When the dead rise, they will neither marry nor be given in marriage; they will be like the angels in heaven."* (Mark 12:25)

Heaven will definitely be heavily populated but it will be a large place. The Apostle John wrote in Revelation the following:

After this I looked and there before me was a great multitude that no one could count, from every nation, tribe, people and language, standing before the throne and in front of the Lamb. They were wearing white robes and were holding palm branches in their hands. (Revelation 7:9)

These are people who have accepted Christ over a period of thousands of years, and the picture we see here is that they are standing before the throne worshipping Jesus Christ, Who is called the Lamb several times in this book.

Heaven will also be a blessed place that we cannot even comprehend at this time. However, as it is written: *"No eye has seen, no ear has heard, no mind has conceived what God has prepared for those who love Him but God has revealed it to us by His Spirit. The Spirit searches all things, even the deep things of God."* (1 Cor. 2:9, 10) We can be assured that this will be a place where God's glory is fully revealed to us. That will truly be something to look forward to! Paul makes another reference to what heaven will be like in another passage: *"Now we see but a poor reflection as in a mirror; then we shall see face to face. Now I know in part; then I shall know fully, even as I am fully known."* (1 Cor. 13:12)

Peter also wrote of the hope that we have and the inheritance that is ours through Jesus Christ.

Praise be to the God and Father of our Lord Jesus Christ! In His great mercy He has given us new birth into a living hope through the resurrection of Jesus Christ from the dead, and into an inheritance that can never perish, spoil or fade—kept in heaven for you, who through faith are shielded by God's power until the coming of the salvation that is ready to be revealed in the last time. (1 Peter 1:3 – 5)

Our God deserves to be praised because of what He has done for us! Notice as well that we through faith are shielded by God's power on a daily basis. That is why we do not have to fear anything that comes our way. It certainly is the reason why I have no fear of death. Our God is in control!

Without going into too many details about heaven (that could be another book!) I do want to share some scriptures from Revelation that will give a little more light about what heaven will be like. Jesus said, *"To him who overcomes, I will give the right to sit with Me on My throne, just as I overcame and sat down with my Father on His throne."* (Revelation 3:21) This demonstrates that we will have a very intimate relationship with our blessed Saviour! We catch a small glimpse of what heaven will be like in the following passage:

Then I saw a new heaven and a new earth, for the first heaven and the first earth had passed away, and there was no longer any sea. I saw the Holy City, the new Jerusalem, coming down out of heaven from God, prepared as a bride beautifully dressed for her husband. And I heard a loud voice from the throne saying, "Now the dwelling of God is with men, and He will live with them. They will be His people, and God Himself will be with them and be their God. He will wipe every tear from their eyes. There will be no more death or mourning or crying or pain, for the old order of things has passed away. He who was seated on the throne said, "I am making everything new!" Revelation 21:1 – 5)

To get a more full picture of what the Holy City will be like, I encourage you to read all of Revelation 21. Its streets will be made of pure gold! The Holy City that will be coming out of heaven will likely be suspended above the new earth. To really find out about these events and what they mean you should become a student of prophesy, for this is what the book of Revelation is about. Those who read this book are called blessed. Truly it is a great blessing.

I have taught the book of Revelation along with the book of Daniel quite a few times in the past, and every time you go through it you gain a greater blessing. God is good, and His power and greatness is shown fully in the book of Revelation.

There is another passage I would like you to see with regards to what heaven will be like. After this, there will be no doubt who you belong to. *"They will see His face, and His name will be on their foreheads. There will be no more night. They will not need the light of a lamp or the light of the sun, for the Lord God will give them light. And they will reign for ever and ever."* (Revelation 22:4, 5)

The "they" that is talked about here are those who have been redeemed by the shed blood of Christ. I would love to have His name etched into my forehead, for I want the world to know that I belong to Him, no matter what my condition on this earth will be like in the coming days and months. Also notice that these people will reign with Christ! I love the topic of Christ's return and heaven. The next chapter will be on His second coming, so you can look for more information concerning when He is returning in that chapter.

Talking about heaven is a tremendous blessing, because it takes our focus off of our mortal bodies and our situation that we find ourselves in on this earth. My total trust is in our Lord Jesus Christ and the promises of future glory that are found in the scriptures. What I have done is given you a glimpse of what the scriptures say about heaven, but please understand that there are many more scriptures on that topic. Jesus, for example, often talked about heaven through parables that He gave when He was on earth. Books on prophesy give more insight than what I could give in the one chapter that I am giving for this.

When you think about heaven and the inheritance that belongs to each believer, there is no need to be concerned about the life we face. Certainly my body does not give me much hope any more, except that I do believe the Lord will heal me. The focus on heaven is important to me because I might not have a long time left on this earth if the Lord does not heal me very soon. Heaven is a great topic to think about at any time because we as believers are called "citizens" of heaven even now. It is important that as Christians we have proper priorities in our lives at all times – that we focus on God and His Kingdom rather that trying to set up our own kingdoms here on this earth.

I might point out, though, that I will be giving another update on my condition in Chapter 12. As I have stated previously, even as I am writing this book my condition is changing to quite an extent with other things propping up almost on a weekly basis. I definitely value every day that God gives me to write this book, because there are some days when I just do not feel up to it because of things that are going on in my body. I need His strength for each day, and I know that He will continue to do that. I am truly thankful to God because He has been faithful to help me in every circumstance, especially since I came down with this disease. I will serve Him with my whole heart as a result of His help to me.

My Unworthiness for His Glory

We must recognize the fact that if Jesus hadn't died on the Cross for our sins, there is no way that we could have been saved. We know from God's Word that *"all have sinned and fall short of the glory of God."* (Romans 3:23) The only way we can see God's glory is if we repent of our sins and ask Christ into our hearts. Sometimes as believers we can go for days before we realize that we have committed sin against God by what we watch on television or what we think of other people. We are to love everyone that we come in contact with, and I wonder if we do that as much as we should.

Do we recognize how transient our lives are in these mortal bodies, and how prone we are to live for ourselves and not for God? We must discipline ourselves daily so that we take the time to devote each day to God and remember that we are nothing in ourselves. Only through Jesus Christ can we be considered worthy of the Kingdom of Heaven. Nothing we can do outside of Christ will earn us the privilege of heavenly glory.

There is no doubt that I fall short in my own walk with Him. I do not spend as much time with Him as I should, even though I have an hour and a half in devotions on most days. Still I need to recognize His greatness more even throughout the day when I am trying to get my own body to perform the way it is supposed to. With all the medication I have to take (some before food and some after food) I do have to discipline myself. However, I also have to discipline myself to bring glory to God even in the most difficult of situations that I find myself in. It is something that I work with constantly.

There is a real temptation for me to complain about the way my body feels, and to focus on my body when others are visiting me. Instead of doing that I need to give glory to the God Who sustains me and gives me life each and every day. He is always there to comfort me and to help me in every situation.

Pride of course is one of the biggest tools that Satan uses in drawing people away from God. When we become proud of what we have done on this earth, we take glory away from God Who gave us that success in the first place. Pride was Satan's biggest downfall as an archangel of God's. It caused his fall and brought about his evil schemes against God in the age in which we are now living (see Isaiah 14:12 – 15 and Ezekiel 28:12 – 17 for descriptions concerning Satan). Pride is also what keeps us away from God when we should be honouring Him instead of taking the praise for ourselves.

Understand that God wants first place in our lives. If we do not give Him first place and live for Him each day, we are not considered worthy of Him. We must love Him enough to even die for His sake if necessary. It is time for all of us, including myself to get our priorities where they belong. We might have to make some serious adjustments in our life, if we are going to live the way Jesus told us to.

Humility, which is the opposite of pride, is what we need mostly in our lives. We must come to the recognition that without God's help we can do nothing. When you get into the kind of situation that I am in, it doesn't take long to arrange your priorities the way you should, especially if you want God's healing touch on your body.

We should not focus solely upon God just because we want Him to heal us. We need to focus on Him simply because we love Him and want Him to have first place in our lives. Healing will come if that is His will for us, but our motives have to be correct.

The Unworthiness That is Felt Because of Christ

There are examples of people who felt unworthy of the ministry they had with Christ and the position they achieved because of Christ. The first example is that of John the Baptist who had this to say about Christ, Who was going to begin His ministry soon. John said: *"I baptize you with water for repentance. But after me will come One Who is more powerful than I, Whose sandals I am not fit to carry. He will baptize you with the Holy Spirit and with fire."* (Matthew 3:11) John the Baptist had been baptising people for the remission of sins, and was therefore the forerunner to Christ's ministry. John later said in talking about Jesus, *"He must become greater; I must become less."* (John 3:30) What John was speaking about certainly should be the kind of feelings that we should express regarding our work for Christ, or even how we live this life. Christ must have first place!

A second example of humility and having the right attitudes about Christ are found in the writings of the Apostle Paul, who said, "*For I am the least of the apostles and do not even deserve to be called an apostle, because I persecuted the church of God.*" (1 Corinthians 15:9) Paul in his lifetime had done a tremendous amount of work for God. He had started churches throughout most of the known world. Yet he did not consider himself worthy to be called an apostle because in the beginning he persecuted the early Christians.

At the same time, we have to be concerned about taking pride in the fact that we have received a certain amount of responsibility and earned certain titles. In my case I was a pastor and a principal for four different schools. However, I cannot take credit for this, because it was God who put me into those positions.

I just had to work hard in each of those positions to bring glory to God. As I wrote in Chapter One how what happens to me now with this disease is that a lot of things bring humility to me. From this perspective, that is not so bad, because I can then bring glory to God. If I decrease, then He can increase in my life, and hopefully receive glory because of my life. He deserves all the glory that we can give to Him.

The Example of Christ

It is interesting that in Heaven He does and will continue to receive glory. He is worthy of all the glory that He can receive. Again by reading Paul's writings we can read about the kinds of attitudes that we should have. This is a tremendous portion of scripture.

> *Do nothing out of selfish ambition or vain conceit, but in humility consider others better than yourselves. Each of you should look not only to your own interests, but also to the interests of others. Your attitude should be the same as that of Christ Jesus: Who, being in very nature God, did not consider equality with God something to be grasped, but made Himself nothing, taking the very nature of a servant, being made in human likeness. And being found in appearance as a man, He humbled himself and became obedient to death— even death on a cross! Therefore God exalted Him to the highest place and gave Him the name that is above every name, that at the name of Jesus every knee should bow, in heaven and on earth and under the earth, and every tongue confess that Jesus Christ is Lord, to the glory of God the Father. (Philippians 2: 3 – 11)*

Do we consciously try to follow Him with the attitudes we maintain? What I wanted you to see in this tremendous passage is the fact that every knee will eventually bow to Jesus and every tongue shall confess that He is Lord. That means that whether or not people accept Him as their Saviour, they will still bow their knee to Him and recognize His lordship over them. The greatest attitude we should have is that of humility. That is what pleases God the most.

There are several passages of scripture in the book of Revelation where Jesus is called worthy. I will share one with you. *"In a loud voice they sang: 'Worthy is the Lamb, who was slain, to receive power and wealth and wisdom and strength and honor and glory and praise!'"* (Rev. 5:12). He truly is worthy of all the praise that we can give to Him! Praise His Name!

You can see that it is imperative that we have the kinds of motives that emulate Jesus Christ if we are going to be suitable to receive the glory that He now has. That is precisely why He died upon the cross for our sins. It is a great privilege that we have to be called children of God and actually sons of God as well. Jesus said that no more would we be called His servants but His friends (John 15:14 – 17). This is amazing when we realize the glory that He now has. May we desire to serve Him with all of our hearts.

What Happens If You Are Not Ready

The Word of God is very clear about the fact that we must accept Jesus Christ as our personal Saviour before we can be ready for heaven. Here are some of the passages in the scriptures that tell us of the necessity of becoming ready. *"Can the Ethiopian change his skin or the leopard its spots? Neither can you do good who are accustomed to doing evil."* (Jeremiah 13:23) We cannot change ourselves enough to make it into the kingdom of God. Certainly you might want to claim that you have done good all of your life, but you cannot get into heaven without accepting Christ as your Saviour. There is absolutely no other way.

Jesus talked about how we can get into heaven on several occasions. One such verse is the following: *"In reply Jesus declared, 'I tell you the truth, no one can see the kingdom of God unless he is born again'."* (John 3:3) He went on in that passage to describe what it means to be born again.

> *Jesus answered, "I tell you the truth, no one can enter the kingdom of God unless he is born of water and the Spirit. Flesh gives birth to flesh, but the Spirit gives birth to spirit. You should not be surprised at my saying, 'You*

must be born again.' The wind blows wherever it pleases. You hear its sound, but you cannot tell where it comes from or where it is going. So it is with everyone born of the Spirit." (John 3:5 – 8)

In order to inherit the Kingdom of God, we must be "born of the Spirit," meaning of course, the Holy Spirit. When Jesus mentioned water, He was referring to being baptised in water. Baptism does not bring salvation, but all who are saved should be baptised in water (baptism means to be fully immersed in water).

Jesus refers to the work of the Spirit as a wind. In other words, when we accept Christ as our Saviour, the Holy Spirit comes into our heart and we are united with God. We don't understand the changes that have taken place within our hearts. The Holy Spirit works in such a way that we are immediately changed.

On the other hand, there are many who will not be ready for Christ's return because, as Jesus said, they are not born again. Jesus said, *"Enter through the narrow gate. For wide is the gate and broad is the road that leads to destruction, and many enter through it. But small is the gate and narrow the road that leads to life, and only a few find it."* (Matt. 7:13, 14) The reason why many cannot find the narrow road is because they do not humble themselves to the point that they repent of their past way of life and accept Christ as their Saviour. It is my hope that all who read this book will be ready for what awaits them after death or for them to be ready when Christ returns.

Judgment for All

Every person who has ever lived on this earth will one day have to face judgment. We read some examples of this in the following passages:

> *Be happy, young man, while you are young, and let your heart give you joy in the days of your youth. Follow the ways of your heart and whatever your eyes see, but know that for all these things God will bring you to judgment.* (Ecclesiastes 11:9)

> *Just as man is destined to die once, and after that to face judgment, so Christ was sacrificed once to take away the sins of many people; and He will appear a second time, not to bear sin, but to bring salvation to those who are waiting for Him.* (Hebrews 9:27)

We all will be judged whether or not we accept Christ as our Saviour. For those that accept Christ as their Saviour and live the kind of lives that God expects of us, here is the judgment that we will face.

So we make it our goal to please Him, whether we are at home in the body or away from it. For we must all appear before the judgment seat of Christ, that each one may receive what is due him for the things done while in the body, whether good or bad. (2 Corinthians 5:9, 10)

This judgment for believers is a judgment for good works. This is explained better in the following passage that Paul wrote for Christians:

For no one can lay any foundation other than the one already laid, which is Jesus Christ. If any man builds on this foundation using gold, silver, costly stones, wood, hay or straw, his work will be shown for what it is, because the Day will bring it to light. It will be revealed with fire, and the fire will test the quality of each man's work. If what he has built survives, he will receive his reward. (1 Corinthians 3:11 – 14)

This is an encouragement for each Christian to live according to God's will for you. Our works will be tested by fire, and only if our works are for God's glory (gold, silver, and costly stones) they will survive and we will be rewarded.

Some, who call themselves Christians because they have accepted Christ, may have done works that will be burnt up. These include works that only satisfy the flesh and are not for God's glory. However, such people will still be saved as long as they acknowledge Christ in their hearts. They will not receive many rewards, however. The "Day" which Paul is writing about is Judgment Day (see Matthew 24). By the way, I am unsure of how many rewards the Lord will give to me on Judgment Day. I do expect to receive rewards for works that have brought glory to God and not to me.

For those who have not accepted Christ as their Saviour, they will be going through the "wide gate" and down the "broad road that leads to destruction" as I wrote above. The Judgment for them, who are many, is found in the passage of scripture which I shared in Chapter Eight. This is Revelation 20:11-15 and it speaks of the White Thrown Judgement. It is a very serious judgement to consider. If you are judged with this judgement, it means that you have gone beyond any chance of accepting Christ as your personal Saviour, and your name is not recorded in the Lamb's Book of Life.

This Judgment is going to be terrible but no one who has not accepted Christ can escape it. If a person knows Christ as His Saviour, his name is written in the Book of Life, and he will have been judged a long time previous to this Judgment. In fact, this White Thrown Judgement is the last of the judgments that will take place at the end of time. The lake of fire is known as the second death and that is reserved for all who are living or have lived without Christ in their lives. This Lake of Fire is a place where the Devil and the Antichrist are thrown into as well. The fire does not destroy the people who are thrown into it because their souls are eternal. They will live in torment forever.

I felt that it was important for me to give this information so that you might get a glimpse of what is ahead you if you are living without Christ as Lord of your life. He can be a tremendous help for those who are living with a fatal disease, but the future that God has planned is far greater than what this life can ever give to us.

Doing All I Can to Serve Him

When we consider our own unworthiness to be able to one day sit by His side, or to talk to Him face to face, it will be automatic for us to fall on our knees before Him and to acknowledge Him as Lord of our lives. He certainly deserves all the praise we can give to Him.

I will with the time that I have left in my present condition, work as hard as I can to write books that I hope will be well received and bring glory to God. I have two books underway at the present time, which I hope to be able to complete. I will be writing until either God takes me home or until I am healed. It is about all that I can do in my present condition, although I can still be an influence for God when people visit me. If God blesses people who read the books that I write, that could be a good ministry for the Lord.

I would like to give you the same verse that I gave you before, when speaking of the fact that being absent from the body means that we will be present with the Lord. Paul wrote, *"So we make it our goal to please Him, whether we are at home in the body or away from it."* (2 Corinthians 5:9) That is truly my goal as well – to please the Lord whether I am here on this earth or if I go home to be with Him.

If God heals me, which I expect will be the case, then things will be different. I will be able to talk again, and I would be very pleased to be able to share what God has done in my life to anyone who would want to listen. We will be much more mobile at that time than we are now. Let me underscore what I just said: I want to serve Him no matter what might happen in my future. He deserves all that I can do for Him!

I would encourage all who read this book to consider what they can do for God, because He certainly is worthy of all that we can do for Him.

May His presence fill all of our lives so that we realize how little time we have left on this earth, and how important it is for us use the time wisely. I am sure that He will be coming soon!

Chapter Eleven:

The Second Coming of Christ

Christ may be coming very soon, this is very exciting time for believers to look forward to. There may not be too much time to spend on this earth even if God is going to heal me.

My burden is to prepare the Church for Christ's coming, and I certainly would be working hard to prepare people for the event if He heals me.

It is important for everyone to understand the days in which we are living. This is as true for believers as well as for those who have not yet come to the faith. Christ is coming soon. Are you ready for his return?

Prophesies Concerning Christ's Coming

We must understand that the Bible has given us several prophecies concerning the coming of Christ. Just as we were given several prophecies concerning His first coming, we have been given even more prophecies concerning His Second coming. Please notice the following prophecies concerning Jesus' birth so many years ago:

> *For to us a child is born, to us a Son is given, and the government will be on His shoulders. And He will be called Wonderful Counselor, Mighty God, Everlasting Father, Prince of Peace. Of the increase of his government and peace there will be no end. He will reign on David's throne and over His kingdom, establishing and upholding it with justice and righteousness from that time on and forever. The zeal of the LORD Almighty will accomplish this.* (Isaiah 9:6, 7)

Notice that was a prophecy about the first coming of Christ. It also predicted   which family He would be a part of – David. That came to pass. Therefore we can understand that prophecies given in the Bible come to pass.

There were several other prophecies – in fact I previously had told you that Christ fulfilled 34 prophecies during His life here on earth. I give you this information to demonstrate to you that the Word of God is true. You can also understand that the prophecies about His Second Coming are also true.

The Nearness of Christ's Return

The importance of everyone who reads this book is that we realize Christ's return is very imminent. He is at hand. That is why in the rest of this chapter I have given several signs (predictions) about Christ's return the second time to the Earth. He is coming soon, so it is important for all who read this book to be ready for His return. The Bible is very clear about laying out the promises of His return, so we must do what we can to become ready for His coming. The main thing for that is to accept Him as your Lord and Saviour. If you do so, you will be ready!

Why I Feel I Must Write About Christ's Return

The fact that Christ is returning soon is an exciting fact for every Christian, but it will be a terrible time for those who refuse to accept Christ into their hearts. From my perspective with this fatal disease, it means that if God will be calling me home pretty soon, I won't have to wait very long before I will be seeing the rest of my family, including all who have accepted Christ as Saviour. If God does heal me, it will mean that I have to move quickly to convince many of the fact that Jesus is returning soon. I have a deep burden for the Church these days to help believers to prepare for Christ's return.

There are many signs that have been fulfilled with regards to Christ's return to this Earth. When He does come to take believers away from this earth, there will be what the Bible calls the Great Tribulation, which will be a holocaust as far as this world is concerned. Because of that, I do want to warn all who read this book that they need to accept Him as Saviour so that they will be ready to meet Him when He returns. He will be coming back to take His family of believers to heaven. I discussed the passage for you in the last chapter, which deals with the Rapture (this was 1 Thessalonians 4:13 -18).

The Bible is very clear that there is a timetable by which Christ has set out for us to get some kind of idea when He will be returning. As to the day and the hour of His return, no one knows that. He will come very suddenly and it will be a surprise for those who are not ready for His return.

I used to feel that Christ would be coming back during my lifetime. He still could do that, but when I was talking about this, I had thought that I would live for about twenty more years on this earth.

Obviously with this fatal disease I probably won't live that long unless God heals me. Between now and 2025, a lot of changes will take place that will lay the groundwork for Christ's return.

I will begin by showing you some signs that will lead to Christ's return. I might point out that in the book entitled, The Spotted and Wrinkled Church which I will finish if the Lord gives me time to do that, I spent two chapters in discussing signs about Christ's return. That of course is in much greater detail that what I will do in this chapter. However in this chapter, I will show you that in truth we are living in what the Bible calls "the Last Days." This is a term that suggests that we are approaching the end of this present age (which is called the Age of Grace). I hope you will enjoy reading about how we can know that these are the last days, all of which point to return of our Lord and Saviour, Jesus Christ. I included this chapter in this book because I know that some who read this book may not know the Lord, and you need to be informed of what to look for when Christ returns. I really want to inform you of what will probably be happening now and in the future.

Signs of His Coming Being Fulfilled

There are several signs that have been fulfilled as far as prophecies are concerned and I will share these with you very briefly.

False Christs and False Prophets

Christ warned us about this three times in the first twenty-four verses in Matthew 24. It is something that must be very important to consider because of the emphasis He put upon it. The fact is that there have never been so many cults around the world as there are today. There are thousands of people in the world today who are calling themselves "Jesus Christ." We have this warning from Jesus:

> *"At that time if anyone says to you, 'Look, here is the Christ!' or, 'There he is!' do not believe it. For false Christs and false prophets will appear and perform great signs and miracles to deceive even the elect—if that were possible. See, I have told you ahead of time."* (Matthew 24:23 – 25)

I believe very strongly that the Rapture of the Church will come before the Tribulation begins. (There are several who have different beliefs such as the middle or end of the Tribulation.) That will be the first phase of His return, and no one besides believers will see Him, because our bodies will be transformed and we will rise to meet Him in the air. At this time He will not touch the earth, but we shall see His glory in an instant of time.

For non-Christians, this will mean the disappearance of their Christian friends and relatives. It will also cause a lot of disasters because many Christians will be driving cars or flying aircraft when suddenly they disappear.

Everyone will see the second phase of Christ's return. Jesus said the following: *"So if anyone tells you, 'There he is, out in the desert,' do not go out; or, 'Here he is, in the inner rooms 'do not believe it. For as lightning that comes from the east is visible even in the west, so will be the coming of the Son of Man."* (Matthew 24:26, 27) At that time everyone on earth will see Christ. The prophet Zachariah wrote that He would stand on the Mount of Olives:

> *Then the LORD will go out and fight against those nations, as He fights in the day of battle. On that day His feet will stand on the Mount of Olives, east of Jerusalem, and the Mount of Olives will be split in two from east to west, forming a great valley, with half of the mountain moving north and half moving south.* (Zechariah 14:3, 4)

Notice that when He comes a great earthquake will take place. Everyone will see Him! I have said this to counter those that claim to be Christ. Do not believe such heresy! Be a student of the Word of God so that you will not be misled.

The Increase of Wars

Jesus said, *"You will hear of wars and rumours of wars, but see to it that you are not alarmed. Such things must happen, but the end is still to come."* (Matthew 24:6) There have been a great amount of wars in this world. The continent that has had the most is Africa. Many of the countries there have had civil wars.

Wars have been increasing exponentially over the last century. But also we can understand that as times passes, the weapons have become much more dangerous, causing a great many more people to die. We see new technology brings more deaths in a war; non-combatants are killed more than ever before. (Just think of the atom bombs that were dropped on two cities in Japan.)

This shows that the sign that Jesus gave is being fulfilled as never before. Statistics I have seen demonstrate how the problems of war have been increasing. For example, major wars numbered <u>19</u> from 1900 to 1945. Between 1945 and 1975 there were <u>119</u> wars. Since then there have been numerous other wars, not including those in the continent of Africa. There has been the Vietnam War, the Russian war with Afganistan, the American war against Iraq, the UN approved war led by the United States against Afganistan, and the allied war against Iraq.

These last two wars are still being waged in the form of terrorist activity in both of these countries. What I have given you is just a smattering of major wars since 1975. Be assured that each war that is fought causes death for many more of the public. The modern wars have become rather against terrorists than against countries. However many countries have been affected by the actions of terrorists including Russia, Britain, Japan, Israel, Canada, and the United States. War is a common topic in many countries around the world today. This sign has certainly been fulfilled in this time in which we are living.

Famines

Jesus said: "*Nation will rise against nation, and kingdom against kingdom. There will be famines and earthquakes in various places.*" (Matthew 24:7) The problem of famine has to do with the population explosion in many of the poorer countries. Famine is a huge problem in the third world countries today. We see advertisements almost every day on television asking for money to help feed children who are starving. It truly is a tremendous problem which grows every day because of the growth of populations. Most countries do not have organized birth control programs to help the situation. This prediction by Jesus is fulfilled today like it never has been in the past.

Earthquakes

In the verse above Jesus also spoke of the increase of earthquakes "in various places."

I have seen statistics that confirm the increase of the numbers of earthquakes from 1948 until 1976. In 1948 the U.S. Government Department of the Interior listed <u>620</u> major earthquakes. Each year the numbers of earthquakes increased so that by 1976 there were <u>7180</u> earthquakes recorded. To give an example of how the incidence of earthquakes has increased recently it has been reported that in the months of January and February of 2004, there were twenty-four severe earthquakes (above 6.0).[30]

We have had more severe earthquakes in Turkey, Indonesia, and California. We hear of more earthquakes each month or sometimes even weekly. The earth is truly *"groaning as in the pains of childbirth right up to the present time."* (Romans 8:22) This is another sign that has been fulfilled. We can expect to see earthquakes where we have never seen them before. Certainly there are faults in places that have not had earthquakes before.

Mistreatment of the Jews

Matthew 24 is mostly aimed at the Jews and the persecution they will face during the Tribulation period of time. Jesus said regarding His people: *"Then you will be handed over to be persecuted and put to death, and you will be hated by all nations because of Me."* (Matthew 24:9) The Jews have indeed been hated by all nations especially during the twentieth century. Even countries such as England and France did not respond positively to the Jews in the time between the two world wars. They have been persecuted tremendously, and their greatest persecution of course was the holocaust during the Second World War. They were hated by the Romans in the first century and have been disliked by people in most of the countries that they migrated to. The Arab countries that surround Israel hate the Jews who now are back in their own country.

Propagation of the Gospel

Jesus said, *"And this gospel of the kingdom will be preached in the whole world as a testimony to all nations, and then the end will come."* (Matthew 24:14) Even though there are groups of people who have never heard the gospel, still every country in the world has at least one Christian living in it.[31] Also the gospel is being preached in countries that only 20 years ago

---

[30] "Whole lotta shakin' going on." Online Traders Web Alliance (www.otwa.com/community/showthread.php.) (May, 2004)

[31] "Global Christianity – A vibrant Christianity is sweeping much of the world…" Evangelical Fellowship of Canada, 2002. (http://www.faithtoday.ca/article_viewer.asp?Article_ID). Material taken from World Christian Encyclopedia.

were closed to the gospel. There have been major revivals in China, Latin America, and among Arab countries in Northern Africa. Again, Christ's prediction, in my mind at least, is being fulfilled.

The Increase of Knowledge and Increased Travel

It is interesting that Daniel, a prophet who lived around 2600 years ago, predicted that in the end times there would be a great increase in knowledge and in travel. We have that prediction in the following verse: "*But you, Daniel, close up and seal the words of the scroll until the time of the end. Many will go here and there to increase knowledge.*" (Daniel 12:4) We are now at that stage in history. No one was able to travel like we do today, and no one could learn as much as we do today. This is quite a remarkable time when you think about it. At the beginning of the twentieth century for example, men were learning about driving a car. A few years beyond the middle of the century, people were going to the moon. At the beginning of the century most people never went to school for twelve years. Now parents expect their children to go to university or other post - secondary institutions after high school. This is a sign that certainly is fulfilled. In other words, we are living in the end-times.

The Nation of Israel

I mentioned a little while ago about the persecution of the Jews. Well, probably one of the greatest signs of our times is the fact that the nation of Israel, which was ended in the year 70 A.D., has now become a nation once more on May 14, 1948. Israel had to become a nation before many of the prophecies could be fulfilled. Jesus taught about a very important event concerning the nation of Israel, which most Bible scholars agree with.

> *Now learn this lesson from the fig tree: As soon as its twigs get tender and its leaves come out, you know that summer is near. Even so, when you see all these things, you know that it is near, right at the door. I tell you the truth, this generation will certainly not pass away until all these things have happened.* (Matthew 24:32-34)

Most scholars, including myself, feel that with the reference to the fig tree Jesus is talking about the nation of Israel. As I mentioned, it became a nation once more in May of 1948. Jesus said this generation would not pass away before He returns to this earth, meaning that people who were born around this time would live to see Christ return. I was born in 1946; that is why I expected to live until He returns. This demonstrates that we are very close to the day of His return to this world!

Signs in the Social World

We read the following scripture in Paul's writing to Timothy:

But mark this: There will be terrible times in the last days. People will be lovers of themselves, lovers of money, boastful, proud, abusive, disobedient to their parents, ungrateful, unholy, without love, unforgiving, slanderous, without self-control, brutal, not lovers of the good, treacherous, rash, conceited, lovers of pleasure rather than lovers of God— having a form of godliness but denying its power. Have nothing to do with them. (2 Timothy 3:1 – 5)

This is a pretty clear commentary that fits in well with what our society is about today. Our society is based on humanism that makes them *"lovers of themselves, lovers of money, boastful and proud."* This is what most people in our society are thinking like today.

Many children today are disobedient to their parents, as they have learned from humanistic teaching how to raise their children. Every phrase could be compared with what is going on today, but I won't take the time to discuss it all. However there is one phrase that I think has to be mentioned because it fits in with our society so well. That is the phrase, *"lovers of pleasure rather than lovers of God."* People today certainly love pleasure more than they love God. Just look at the importance of sports in our society today. People love to create sports idols on Sundays instead of worshipping the true God.

Spiritist Manifestations

We are living in an age in which the New Age is becoming important to people who influence many others. The New Age brings with it demons and spirits which are not from God. The Apostle Paul had things to say about this as well. *"The Spirit clearly says that in later times some will abandon the faith and follow deceiving spirits and things taught by demons.*

Such teachings come through hypocritical liars, whose consciences have been seared as with a hot iron." (1Timothy 4:1,2)

There are many who used to be followers of Christ who have now joined in cultist activities and in the New Age movement. By the way, the New Age is going to be the main church that is spoken about in the Book of Revelation. It will be a combination of various churches, all under the New Age umbrella. In the New Age, old gods such as those of the Egyptians and Babylonians are very popular. Those "gods" are no more than deceiving spirits that Paul wrote about. Notice that people who are hardened to the gospel have in many cases, had their "consciences seared" as Paul wrote about. They are now willing to do anything that they would like to do, whether it is good or bad.

Lawlessness

Lawlessness has greatly increased in almost every major city in North America. Paul wrote about this in the following way: "*For the secret power of lawlessness is already at work; but the One who now holds it back will continue to do so till He is taken out of the way.*"(2 Thessalonians 2:7) It is interesting that the King James Version of the Bible presents this verse in the following way: "*For the mystery of iniquity doth already work: only he who now letteth will let, until he be taken out of the way.*" The "mystery of iniquity" is something that I will be writing about as a sign of Christ's soon return a little later in this chapter.

It is believed that the One holding back the tide of lawlessness is the Holy Spirit, who is the Third Person of the Trinity. He will be taken out of the way when the Church is raptured into Heaven. Today there is a strong pull that some people feel they should break the law. Often drug addiction is involved with lawlessness today. Lawlessness takes center stage in almost every newscast that we hear from the media. The mystery of iniquity is hard at work today! Again, this prophecy is right for the days we are currently living in.

Falling Away From the Faith

Jesus warned of people falling away from the faith in these last days. He said: "*Because of the increase of wickedness, the love of most will grow cold, but he who stands firm to the end will be saved.*" (Matthew 24:12, 13) We can see that this indeed is happening in several churches today. People are more compelled to going to churches that are popular instead of asking

God where they should go. The love of many has been growing cold, and as I mentioned earlier some of those who are falling away get involved in cults instead, where the gospel is perverted through the ideas of certain people. Jesus said that those who stand firm will be saved. Therefore it is important to have a strong faith whether you are dying from a fatal disease or not. We must have a strong testimony for God in these last days.

There is another passage, which warns us not to be deceived. *"Don't let anyone deceive you in any way, for (that day will not come) until the rebellion occurs and the man of lawlessness is revealed, the man doomed to destruction."* (2 Thessalonians 2:3) There are other verses following this verse that discusses the "man of lawlessness" more fully. Just for your interest, the man of lawlessness is a man who will claim to be God. He is known as the Antichrist and one day He will rule the entire world for a short period of time.

Notice from this last verse that the Antichrist will be known as the man of lawlessness. Even now Satan's spirit is in the hearts of many who wish to destroy the lives of others. They are prone to do evil, and not good. It is true that some of these people used to be Christians. According to what Jesus said there will be many who will fall away from the faith. There will be many saved during the Tribulation, but they will probably have to die for their faith. Therefore do not wait until the Tribulation comes to accept Christ into your life!

Empty, Powerless Religion

In the passage that I gave to you from 2 Timothy, there is an important phrase at the end of it which talks about religion that exists today. It says that some will be *"lovers of pleasure rather than lovers of God—having a form of godliness but denying its power."* (2 Timothy 3:5) That is what some churches are like today. They have a form of godliness (notice that it is only a form i.e. rituals) but they know nothing of God's power to transform their lives and free them of sin.

Another passage is found in Revelation and talks about lukewarm churches, which is typical of such churches today.

> *To the angel of the church in Laodicea write: These are the words of the Amen, the faithful and true witness, the ruler of God's creation. I know your deeds, that you are neither cold nor hot. I wish you were either one or the other! So, because you are lukewarm—neither hot nor cold—I am about to*

spit you out of my mouth. You say, 'I am rich; I have acquired wealth and do not need a thing.' But you do not realize that you are wretched, pitiful, poor, blind and naked. (Rev. 3:14 – 17)

There are many who apply the letters to Churches in chapters two and three of Revelation to the Church Age, with each letter applying to the historical churches throughout the ages. It is interesting that what was written to the Laodicean church applies to the Church Age in which we are living today. I believe this to be true because Chapter Four of Revelation moves the church to heaven. The Church is no longer mentioned as being on the ground in the rest of that book. This shows that God knows what this Age is all about, particularly in North America. The religion in many churches today is lukewarm or cold altogether. This is another sign that is fulfilled today!

The Mystery of Iniquity

This sign relates to how long God will wait before He steps in to judge the world as He does in the Great Tribulation that is about to come on this earth. Be warned that this will be such a bad time on earth that Jesus said this about them: *"For then there will be great distress, unequalled from the beginning of the world until now—and never to be equalled again. If those days had not been cut short, no one would survive, but for the sake of the elect those days will be shortened."* (Matthew 24:21, 22) This demonstrates how horrible those days will be.

Therefore, we have to estimate whether or not this world has achieved that level of iniquity to this point in history. Notice what God told Abraham in the book of Genesis. *"In the fourth generation your descendants will come back here, for the sin of the Amorites has not yet reached its full measure."* (Genesis 15:16) God was telling Abraham that His descendents would be going to Egypt and would be there for four generations, (they were actually there for 430 years) signifying that God knew how long it would take for the iniquity of the Amorites to be so bad that God would tell His people to destroy them totally.

Jesus told us,

No one knows about that day or hour, not even the angels in heaven, nor the Son, but only the Father. As it was in the days of Noah, so it will be at the coming of the Son of Man. For in the days before the flood, people were eating and drinking, marrying and giving in marriage, up to the day Noah entered the ark; and they knew nothing about what would happen until the flood came and took them all away. That is how it will be at the coming of the Son of Man. (Matthew 24:36 – 39)

The question that is important is this: has the level of iniquity in this age reached the level of iniquity that existed in the days that Noah lived? We have done some very terrible things in this age, including abortions, and a total disrespect for law that we talked about a little while ago. Also, our Canadian government is focussing upon legalizing the marriages of homosexuals and lesbians. This is another step towards completing the level of iniquity in Canada!

God is waiting for the level of iniquity to increase to a certain level so that He would be totally just in bringing the Tribulation upon them. This is an interesting topic that I will be discussing more fully in the other book that I am writing.

Other Signs

I have given you fourteen different signs, which will indicate when the world will be ready for Christ to return to this earth, this time in judgment. There are several other signs, some of which I will mention briefly here.

Many people feel that one of the first prophesies that will herald the end of the Age of Grace will be a war between Russia who will be allied with several Arab countries against the small nation of Israel. This is found in Bible prophesy in the book of Ezekiel. You can read it in Chapters 38 and 39 of Ezekiel. By the way, Chapter 37 is an account of Israel once again becoming a country. It is called the Valley of Dry Bones. Here is a passage from Ezekiel 38:

> *The word of the LORD came to me: "Son of man, set your face against Gog, of the land of Magog, the chief prince of Meshech and Tubal; prophesy against him and say: 'This is what the Sovereign LORD says: I am against you, O Gog, chief prince of Meshech and Tubal. I will turn you around, put hooks in your jaws and bring you out with your whole army—your horses, your horsemen fully armed, and a great horde with large and small shields, all of them brandishing their swords. Persia, Cush and Put will be with them, all with shields and helmets, also Gomer with all its troops, and Beth Togarmah from the far north with all its troops—the many nations with you."*
>
> *"Get ready; be prepared, you and all the hordes gathered about you, and take command of them. After many days you will be called to arms. In future*

years you will invade a land that has recovered from war, whose people were gathered from many nations to the mountains of Israel, which had long been desolate. They had been brought out from the nations, and now all of them live in safety. " (Ezekiel 38:1 – 8)

This is a very accurate picture of Israel as the country that others will be fighting against. From the countries given, these are peoples of the far north such as Russia and other countries around the Black Sea. Some Muslim countries today will be involved as well. This means that Russia probably will become a totalitarian government soon and would join forces with some Muslim countries.

The Muslim countries have already been involved with wars with Israel, so that wouldn't be hard to accept. This is called the **Battle of Gog and Magog**. If you continue reading in this chapter in Ezekiel you will find that the invaders will be destroyed by God directly, Who steps in to help Israel. By the way horses will probably not be used as the scriptures indicate. Modern weapons of warfare were not understood then.

Another sign is the formation of what could be called the Revised Roman Empire, which will involve not only the European Common Market but also the entire world that will be divided up into ten sections (this is shown in the Book of Daniel). Therefore it is important to look at the treaties that have been formed to date, such as the one Europe has, and also the treaty (NAFTA) that involves all of North America and probably soon all of South America. These types of treaties that will involve the entire world could be established after the Church is raptured to heaven.

There are several more things that will take place in the future – such as a society that will be free from money and one credit card that will be for everything (for your interest, Singapore is now trying this out). While I do not have much time to discuss these now, these are something for us to keep our eyes open for. This could also take place after the Rapture takes place.

It is exciting to look at how Bible prophecies have been fulfilled. God's Word is true, and all prophesies either has been already met (as many are fulfilled now) with others to be fulfilled soon in the future. It is also interesting that, for those considering whether or not Jesus truly is God's Son, when Jesus came to earth the first time, throughout His life and His death He fulfilled **thirty-four** prophecies. That is amazing when you think about it. You should realize then that God's Word is inspired!

My Personal Interest in Christ's Second Coming

As you can probably tell from what I have written in this chapter, I love to study God's Word and the prophesies that I find there. I have long been a student of the Word, and as I previously have mentioned I have taught the Book of Daniel as well as the Book of Revelation several times. I also created a course on the New Age Movement that I taught in Bible College. I have also taught shorter versions of the course in churches at different times. As a result, I have been excited about the return of Christ to this world and the Great Tribulation that will follow His return.

With this fatal disease, that I hope the Lord will heal me of, I probably won't live long enough to see Him return. However I will be coming with Him to the Rapture of the Church, which I will be praising Him for. It will truly be something to view the condition of this world from God's point of view. He is not only the Creator of the world but also Jesus is also going to be the Judge over everyone - the righteous as well as the unrighteous. I much rather be able to have Him judge me for my good works than judge me because my name is not found in the Book of Life!

Really though, we do not know what our roles in Heaven will be if we die before He comes again. There are millions of holy people in heaven already, so it will be God who assigns us work. I expect to be busy in heaven! We have a great responsibility to live in such a way on this earth that we will be ready for the Lord's return. It is my hope that everyone who reads this book will make themselves ready!

Chapter Twelve:
An Update on My Condition

It has been my plan to have updates throughout my chapters so that you could see how this disease is progressing. I originally finished my book in June so that would have been sufficient. However, it is now October, and my condition has had a tremendous amount of changes taking place. As I began this book, the first chapter talked about what A.L.S. has been like, and how it has been progressing. Now towards the end of the book I'll give you this chapter to show some of the final stages in its development.

What I am saying in the chapter is that if the Lord really wants to heal me, now is the time for Him to do so, because I definitely do not have very much time left in my life here on Earth. The changes that have taken place are quite extensive, which I will show you in this chapter.

An Update until June 2005

I now have a biPap machine and I have spent one night in the Intensive Care Unit at the Misercordia Hospital to have the machine set to what I need. I have had some problems with it but I now feel that they have been worked out, and I have been able to get a good sleep for most of this week. Part of the problem was in getting some medications that will help me sleep better, and that has now been given to me.

Meanwhile in the last three weeks in May, I have had some rather different problems. I have found out that there are three reasons for me to be coughing:

1) Aspirating my own saliva;

2) Congestion in my lungs; and

3) Not getting enough oxygen into my lungs and not being able to expel carbon dioxide out of my lungs.

It seems that all three have been active during the last month to a certain extent.

Also in the last month I have experienced something that is quite new for A.L.S. patients. I received radiation treatments from the Cross

Cancer Institute in Edmonton. It meant taking radiation treatments on some salivary glands five days in a row. As a result my skin on each side of my face next to my ears became very sensitive, and very sensitive to the sunshine. The results were supposed to be apparent in ten or fifteen days, which means now. However there has been other circumstances arising that meant I had to take more medication.

Two weeks ago, I developed a sore throat so I went to see my doctor. He took a swab and found that I had a strep throat infection. I suppose I got that because of the radiation I received. Also, there can be a lot of build –up of bacteria in my mouth even though I brush my teeth four times a day and take antiseptic mouthwash the same number of times. I was just over that when I received severe pain in my right foot. Concerned that it might have been the spread of A.L.S. to my limbs, we went to see my doctor for the second week in a row. It turned out to be gout, which was extremely painful and probably caused by my limbs not getting enough oxygen. My doctor also checked out my lungs and found that there was an infection in my right lung. All of these problems needed more medication for me. Some medication I had to take before I had my feeding and some after I fed myself.

With the extra medication, it meant that I had to take much more water to clean my tube out before and after I fed myself my food. I was therefore taking around five more syringes of liquids than the minimum limits I was supposed to take. When I take a bunch of water, this adds to my supply of saliva, and I could not really tell if the radiation treatments did any good. Now though, things are settling down, and the amount of medication I have to take is greatly diminished again. So far, I have been able to reduce one form of anti-saliva medication.

In taking the antibiotic for my lung infection, one morning I had a big coughing spell in which I coughed up a lot of phlegm from my lung. My right lung is now clear, and I hope it will stay that way for a long time in the future. The fact that our doctor discovered it soon enough so that I got it looked after before pneumonia set in again was a blessing. With all of this, I truly thank God for my doctor, who is a strong Christian who prays for me at each visit. I am also very thankful to God for the fact that I can get off the large amount of medication that I was taking.

It is my hope that I won't continue getting such infections that I have had this month, knowing that those sorts of things truly slow up my improvement and the work that I want to get done. I am now back to coughing very little so I hope that will continue to be the case for me.

Because of the fact that my saliva was not cut back as much as it should have, in the middle of June I had to go back for some more radiation treatments. According to the doctor that I go to see at the Cross Cancer Institute, the glands that are being shut down with the radiation treatments, means that seventy per cent of my saliva should be eliminated. To me this is very good news! I hope that this does become true in my case.

The radiation that was done this time was focused upon two other glands, which are on each side of my face. After the first day, I could find a change in the amount of saliva that I had. However, I also realized that what I had left was not really saliva but mucous instead.

Though a nurse at the Cross Cancer Institute said this was normal, others were as concerned about this as I was. This became a big source of coughing for me, because I had a tendency of gagging over the mucous. I was very fortunate, however, in that the respiratory therapist, who comes to see me on a weekly basis, had introduced me to a nebulizer. The drug Salbatamol Dr. Myrholm prescribed for me initially was supposed to keep my lungs from becoming infected with pneumonia. It means that I will be coughing up phlegm quite a bit, and that is not too nice a situation.

Dr. Myrholm also gave me Acetylcysteine that would go through the nebulizer to make the mucous much thinner. This did thin out the mucous but it also caused me to cough a great deal. I coughed so much that my throat became sore. Therefore Dr. Myrholm introduced another drug to me with the suspicion that I was getting much thicker mucous possibly because of excretions coming from my sinus glands. Genbudesonide was a drug that I sprayed into my nose, and it seems to have the desired affect.

However, to stem the coughing that I had because of too much saliva in my mouth, I decided to go back on anti-saliva medication – Amitriptylline and Glycoprrolate at noon. I am now taking it only twice a day at the maximum (sometimes I do not need it) and in smaller quantities than previously. This has cut down my coughing considerably and made me much more able to function as I did before.

The doctor had predicted that, with the radiation treatments, the saliva would be cut down by seventy per cent. And that is the case. However, the thirty per cent is still too much for me so I have to keep taking limited amounts of anti-saliva medication.

As a result of the latest round of radiation treatments; I found that it did quite a round on me starting with the first treatment. My cheeks became very swollen and remained that way all of the week. Even into the next week, the swelling did not go away completely and the cheeks were now becoming more sensitive each day. It meant that I really have to be careful going outside in the sunshine because my face could get sunburned very easily. But something happened during this time (late in June and early in July) that is hard to explain. I don't know if it was the result of the last round of radiation or if this had something to do with the progression of the disease.

Rather Sudden Developments of the Disease

I was going through a rather difficult time for the last three weeks, so this is what I recorded on paper, so that I could put it into this book:

> I have been fighting with depression over the last three weeks. (My wife feels that this might just be the progression of the disease because I was not showing many signs of depression during this time.) I guess it started with the last radiation treatments. With all of the things going on in my body I have been thinking that the Lord might be taking me home very soon. I really haven't returned to the way I was feeling before the radiation treatments. I am happy to be able to control my saliva again but I am not feeling as good anymore. I am always tired and I haven't been able to get into the Word the way I want to. My motivation to get things done just isn't there anymore, and I have lost a lot of my energy. I have to work hard against my feelings to get things done. Though I love walking, it is difficult for me to do that any more. To me this is a big spiritual battle that I am in right now.

I am now over the feeling of depression, but I still do not have the energy that I previously had. It does mean quite an adjustment for me. One night I had the best sleep that I had for a long time. However when I settled down to read the Word I became very tired. I have come to the conclusion that I will need to have a nap almost every day, so I have to change my schedule quite a bit. By the way, I have always been a person who likes to have a schedule for everything, but now I guess I have to focus more on my body's needs. This is requiring a large amount of adjustment for me.

I am wondering about the progression of the disease in this manner, because my lungs are still functioning pretty well, and my oxygen count is still very good. Why am I therefore getting so tired? This is something I have to ask the experts about.

Equipment That I Am Using

I have been getting a lot of instruments that are mainly supposed to help my lungs. I thought I should review all the machines that I now am using. The first machine of course was the speech synthesizer, which I have to use for almost all of my talking. Secondly, I received a suction machine that I use whenever I get too much saliva or phlegm. Then I received the biPap machine that is supposed to help my breathing. Our respiratory therapist stated that I breathe deeper into my lungs when I use the biPap, which is an interesting result of me using it. Because my right lung is especially weak at the bottom of it, I also received a "Cough Assist" machine that assists me in coughing so that whatever I have in my lungs can be coughed out. However I had problems with coughing deeply in my chest, so we took that back and brought back a manual type of instrument. I have to practice coughing after I have taken a large amount of air into my lungs. As stated in the last paragraph, our respiratory therapist brought me a "nebulizer" and my doctor prescribed some medication for me to take through the machine. The nebulizer changes the medication from liquid to a mist that I breathe into my lungs. It seems to be a very effective machine because it often causes me to cough. Once it caused me to cough up some phlegm, which was very good. You now have a run-down on the machines that I have been using. Hopefully they will assist in keeping me alive!

A Rather Enjoyable Holiday

A lot of things have happened so that now I am wondering if I am at the last stages of my life unless God does soon heal me. It has been quite a road to travel upon.

Everything seemed to be okay throughout the holidays. We went with our family to Victoria, B. C. and then to Parksville, B.C. It was a great time in a house beside the ocean. I could go to the ocean or stay in the house for a rest. It was a very good time, though I had to take my food through a syringe. As a result the syringe did not last very long. It was also difficult to work around the family as they prepared meals for the rest of the family. It was also good to get home. By the way, the traveling wasn't a problem, because my wife and I flew there and our daughter and son-in-law could take various pieces of equipment for me because they traveled there in their car.

Coughing Without Lung Infection

Once we got back, however, my system started to change. Late in August and early in September I began to cough a great deal, so much so that I was staying awake for about nine nights, also keeping my wife awake. I truly thought that this was because I had infection in my chest.

After all, I had suffered two aspirating pneumonias already and my coughing was the same way. However on her weekly visit, our respiratory therapist could not find any crackling in my chest. She found that both of my lungs have an area in the bottom of them that are completely silent – in other words no air was getting to the bottom of my lungs any more.

Our doctor also listened to my lungs and had them take an x-ray to see if I had pneumonia. He couldn't find any pneumonia though he had given me a new antibiotic to take. He also gave me morphine to take which was supposed to control my coughing. The morphine worked wonderfully well. Very soon my coughing had vanished.

However there were some side effects from the morphine. Other than making me very tired, morphine also makes me very constipated. It was a combination of all these things that made me very nauseated so that I vomited up everything out of my stomach on one occasion. I have been wrestling with a variety of things trying to get my bowels working again and finally it looks like that has been accomplished. I was apparently becoming nauseated mostly because of my constipation. This I can tell is going to be a constant struggle.

Meanwhile I feel very weak and my body has degenerated quite a bit. At this point it looks like the end is not very far off unless the Lord decides to heal me. My body is currently acting very tired, partly because of the morphine and partly because of the affects of Bulbar A.L.S.

The use of morphine has changed quite a bit. First of all, I was putting it into my stomach by syringe. Then I was given tablets I could take apart, putting the contents into my stomach twice a day. Now I take morphine into my system through a pump that has to be plugged into an electrical source. The pump would then install morphine into my system (not my stomach) through a needle for twenty-four hours a day.

However, with this information, which is very up to date (October 25, 2005), it could be changing almost on a daily basis because of other complications.

Troubling Family Matters

There are other disasters that came up as well during this time. In June my older brother, Ron, died within fifteen minutes with a massive heart attack. He died after feeling the attack for fifteen minutes. We attended his funeral on June 18 and it was quite a time for me to meet some of my family members and friends that I hadn't seen for a number of years. I had a difficult time keeping my speech synthesizer going until I found a plug that I could use. Then I had friends and relatives come to me so that I could speak to them.

Two months later my nephew died very quickly. He was an epileptic patient who fell into a campfire when he had a seizure. He was 80% burned and died immediately after the machines that were keeping him alive were turned off. This was extremely difficult for his father who is my next oldest brother. He had his brother and his son die two months apart.

These events made me think of eternity. I am glad that God is the judge over these matters and we don't have to be. However, it did make me think of the need to be ready because we can die at any time. My question to you is this – are your ready to meet with God? Are you ready to say goodbye to this world if God decides to take you home? Some of my siblings were wondering why this disease came upon me when I was living a godly life. My answer to that is simply that I am ready to go. I long to see heaven! Also God wants each one to be ready to go.

Palliative Care and What It Means

Palliative Care is specifically for those whose lives are coming to an end soon. Actually, I think in Palliative Care they expect a person to live for a short period of time.

My condition became very serious when I was unable to do the regular routine for myself. Later I found out that the Palliative Care workers did not think I would make it through the weekend. This was a very sobering thought for me but at the time I was so ill that I believed it could definitely be the case. With me it is a day-to-day experience.

It was truly a time for me to need to have others with me always. My wife, who was home for six weeks to recover from surgery, was with me for at least two weeks without leaving my side. I needed round the clock care. The Palliative Care workers were planning on setting up respite care for when Ann went back to work.

After I got on the morphine pump and the new upgraded bipap my condition changed for the good. I have felt much improved for the last five days or so. My strength came back some. I once again am able to do all my routine care. The cough assist has helped me to bring up mucous. We decided that I would not need the respite care at this time. I am thankful to God for the good time He has allowed me to have recently.

How I Felt During The Lowest Part of My Life

During the times when I really felt ill, I took the time to write a note to our family members because I felt that the end was drawing very near. I intended to give this information to our respiratory therapist who visits me at least once a week. This was one day after my birthday.

I include that information here.

My Condition Today, October 13, 2005

This has been one of the worst days for me with regards to the way I have been feeling. I haven't been feeling very good for about one week at least and it is difficult for me to explain why I am feeling so poorly. I have been feeling that I need to be in bed all day or be in the hospital.

This morning when I was brushing my teeth I vomited again, showing that my gag reflexes are increasing once again. Also my jaw has been vibrating quite a bit recently (this is something that goes with A.L.S.). However the vibration hasn't been only with my jaw. For several weeks I have felt this vibration beginning by hearing it in my ears. It is something like hearing a pulse beat within your temple but much faster. Today my left knee got that same vibration in it that my jaw had. I moved my foot and it quit but when I stood on it, it started up again. It has left now when I've been moving around.

Yesterday I got the same feeling in my left arm but it didn't last very long.

My stomach has been a bit upset today, but I took a suppository and had a pretty good-sized bowel movement. This has helped my stomach somewhat.

Generally my body has been feeling very weak and not very cooperative. I am constantly feeling very tired, and not able to get the strength back that I once had. Even to type this has been quite hard for me to do.

I really don't know if there is anything my doctors could do to help me, but I am thinking that I am coming to the end of my life unless the Lord comes to heal me. Our kids had lots a prayer for me last night but I don't know if the Lord is going to heal me or take me home to be with Him. Right now, though I am truly suffering a great deal.

What can be done for me? I hope there is something that can be done, or I will have to spend the rest of my life in bed."

Ann, my wife, included some material here as well so Dr. Myrholm, who was coming to see me, could get this as well.

Change in sleeping pattern:

Before Howard would sleep from 11 p.m. to around 8 a.m. with a few periods of waking up. He would sleep from 3p.m. to 6 p.m. plus sleep some other times during the day. On October 12th and 13th he was unable to sleep hardly at all. He slept from 11p.m. until 3 a.m. then off and on from 3 a.m. until 5 a.m. and was awake the rest of the time both nights. He also tried to sleep many times during the day but was unable to. Having had the morphine increased on October 14th Howard slept very well during the night and also was able to sleep better during the day today. So he is feeling a little better.

This is how I felt for the period of about one week or more. However I then got help from another respiratory therapist, Sonya Wheeler, who works at the Misercordia Hospital. She is the one who specializes in the biPap machine.

New biPap Machine

Sonya Wheeler phoned our place on Wednesday, October 19, suggesting to us that she should update the program on my biPap machine because she could make it so that I could sleep better. Therefore we went to see her on that day and while I rested and even slept for a while on a bed she provided for me in the hospital, she reprogrammed my biPap. In doing so she found something else – that I would stop breathing for a while sleeping (which is called sleep apnea). This meant that I should get another biPap that focuses on this need. It has an invasive quality, meaning that if I stopped breathing, it would force me to breathe.

Sonya also programmed the biPap so that it forces air into my lungs at a higher rate, meaning that oxygen gets into my lungs well. It also forces out the carbon dioxide to a higher degree.

The result is that since I got the new biPap I have been sleeping better – so good in fact, that I have not been sleeping much at all during the day. I have felt much more rested and able to have much more energy. Mind you, if I sit and do nothing for a while, I still can get tired and sleepy. Recently though, my focus has been on getting this book ready for publication. There is not much more left on it to get finished. I thank God for that!

I truly do thank God for the expertise that He has given to people who are health care workers. Such people have been a great help for me. The new biPap has given me new hope for an extended life. It is my hope that my life will continue so that I can get more done on my other book before He truly calls me home.

The Possibility of Respite Care

We have been looking at the probability of me needing respite care when my wife goes back to work once again. There are occasions when I get mucous in my throat and I do need help to get it cleared out. We also got back from Sonya the "Cough Assist" machine, which she had given to me previously, but I had no use for it at that time. Now however, it is very useful in clearing the mucous out of my throat. It does a much better job than the suction machine does, because the only way for me to get mucous out with the suction machine is to vomit it out. Vomiting of course is not a good activity for someone who has the possibility of gaining an aspirating form of pneumonia!

I mention the "Cough Assist" machine because I would need some help to use it, and that could come in the form of respite care.

My wife Ann will have to go to work soon and she should not have to be concerned about leaving me at home. That can be helped by respite care. There are other possible things that turn up almost every morning that could be difficult for me to deal with without someone who can talk for me. For example, this morning the needle for morphine came out of my body and that meant we had to take the machine off until a nurse came here and put a new needle in. Such a person would be impossible for me to phone if I was by myself.

I also am thinking of the time when my body might degenerate to the point where I might need to be in bed for twenty-four hours a day. In that case I definitely would need continuous care and my wife would still have to work. The need for respite care then is very definite at that point.

Birthday Blessings

Remember that I mentioned a little while ago about the birthday that I recently had. Because this could be my last birthday (unless the Lord heals me), Ann had an extended birthday celebration for me.

It was too bad that I was feeling so poorly at the time. However, on my actual birthday, I was presented with a computer plus speakers and carrying cases. This computer is a special laptop that will speak for me as well. I still have the original voice synthesizer. I use that in our bedroom to talk to my wife there. It still works but it always needs to be plugged in because batteries do not last in it.

I was able to get a nice Bible program installed on the laptop, in which a person reads the Bible for me. This is a tremendous asset since I do have difficulty reading the Bible these days (I hope to get back to that soon however.) I can still have God's Word close to me all of the time.

Another nice feature of my birthday celebrations was that almost all of my siblings came to see me the following Sunday morning and had a good visit with me. In the afternoon we went to our daughter's house where we had several friends over as well as my relatives. We had another nice visit there. It was truly a nice birthday celebration!

My Final Question – Is God Still Going to Heal Me?

As you can see my time is drawing very short unless God heals me. In many ways I am looking to go home to be with my Lord. In other ways, my spirit has been down somewhat, all because I haven't been able to spend time in God's Word. I must do what I can to restore the fellowship that I had with Him, though my days are so busy that I don't have much time to be alone with God. One way or another, I would like my suffering to come to an end. I guess only time will tell what God's answer will be.

In the last chapter of this book I have a word for caregivers, my wife has some things to say as my main caregiver, and my message to all is that I hope that all will be ready for Christ's return. Knowing Christ can also help you tremendously in any valley you might be going through. God bless you!

Chapter Thirteen:
Final Comments Plus Caregiver's Thoughts

In this final chapter it is important for me to inform you of what I believe lies ahead for me. This is also a good time for my chief caregiver, my wife Ann, to share with you her feelings. In many ways this is a much harder situation for her than it is for me, so it is important that I give her an opportunity to share what she feels about this entire experience.

Ann is not only the chief caregiver, but she also is responsible for working hard to bring in an income that helps us in our situation. First of all, I will share some of my reflections concerning what I feel is spiritual warfare.

Reflections Concerning the Healing Process

As I began writing this book in January 2005, remember that I was hoping that I would be healed by the time I finished it. However, as you saw from the last chapter, my regression has been steadily going downhill. It is up to God now!

I have asked God on many occasions about what His will is for my life, but He has not yet told me what He wants from me, except for the fact that I need to have faith that He will heal me. Therefore I am planning on that. However, that healing needs to come to me within the next year because this disease is moving very quickly within my body. I certainly hope that I can be healed soon.

There are several people, including myself, who feel that our enemy, the devil, is trying to see me as being finished with my life here on this earth. That means he must be encountered by believers who are interceding for me. It is really spiritual warfare, and my responsibility is not to accept what is going on but instead demonstrating faith that God will heal me. The end result of this experience should be a victorious healing so that God can be glorified by it. I guess we won't see the end result at this time, but God may wait until the last minute to heal me.

There is some interesting things happening with regards to my healing. Several people (including a person who does not know the Lord) have had dreams or visions of me speaking with a clear voice. Why would God give them such dreams or visions if He is not going to heal me? I do feel that since He is showing other people that I am healed, I then will be healed. I hope that healing comes very soon. God would certainly be glorified if He did heal me, and I could spend the rest of my life ministering to others that He would guide me to.

Further Developments to Anticipate

As mentioned before, the bulbar form of A.L.S. moves very quickly compared to the other form. That means death with come more quickly for me if God does not intervene. It is usually the last stage for people who have had the other form of A.L.S. They develop bulbar A.L.S. and then die soon.

Therefore if God chooses not to heal me, I expect that I am truly limited in the time that I have left on this earth. However I have eternity to look forward to with a glorified body that no longer has any form of any disease.

Even this form of bulbar A.L.S. is moving more quickly than usual. As it has been moving into my lungs quickly, I might not have too much time left if I cannot breathe on my own. I do not want to be living a long time if I need a respirator to help me to breathe. Some of this is speculation as of yet because I am not sure how this disease will be progressing in the future. My arms and legs are as strong as always. Doctors check on this regularly, and find this is the case for me.

Regarding future developments, if I am not healed, I would expect that the disease would be spreading to my lungs before it spreads to my arms and legs. As I have mentioned previously, my problems with inhaling air and exhaling carbon dioxide have already developed, and would become more and more severe as time passes. Eventually I would have to wear a biPap mask during the day as well as at night. I also expect that since I would be getting more and more tired as the days go by, I will probably have to take a nap during the day (I seldom have done this in the past) which I have recently done a few times in the last few weeks.

Eventually I would simply go to sleep and not wake up. To me that is a good way to die, but a doctor suggested a worse way. He suggested that I might get a normal type of pneumonia that comes from an ordinary type of influenza. I have had a flu shot and will probably take a shot that is supposed to keep me from getting pneumonia. Getting a regular form of pneumonia could be extremely difficult for me and I could then spend a couple months in an Intensive Care Unit in a hospital. Then, as the doctor suggested, I might need to have an "Invasive Mechanical Ventilation" instrument so that it would help me to breathe until my condition improved. We have stated that I would probably not be using such a device, but as you can see, it depends upon the situation that I am in and the general health that I would have. Invasive Mechanical Ventilation means a tracheotomy would be placed in my throat by surgery.

I have filled in a "Health Care Directive" for people who might come in to give me assistance or for medical personnel. The fact is that the directive can be changed depending upon the condition that I am facing. Right now the directive says that there will be no cardio-pulmonary resuscitation. If I have a heart attack that means the disease is giving trouble there so I will not be resuscitated. At this point we have also stated that I would not want a tracheotomy placed into my throat, but we might want to change that given the situation that I might be in. It is a document that is pretty straight forward so others will know how to treat me. It is also a guideline for my wife so that she won't be working on emotions alone. This document makes it easier for medical personnel to know what should be done in an emergency. It is a directive that is specifically designed for A.L.S. patients.

When this book is published, I might still be alive and God might have healed me. Or possibly I could die of the disease. If either of these happened probably the book would be published again to add an addendum to it stating that I am healed or that I've gone home to be with the Lord. One way or another I would like my readers to be informed. I am waiting on the Lord to heal me so that I could be a strong witness for Him and bring glory to Him. One way or another I will be giving Him praise and worship, whether I am here at this home or if I am in my eternal home in Heaven.

We have decided that if God is going to heal me that my voice would have to improve first because it would be kind of dangerous to check whether God has healed me by eating regular food. As I stated previously, I do not want to die by choking if at all possible. He could do it all instantly or He could do it gradually, depending on what He desires me to do.

Ready For God's Plans to be Fulfilled

My wife is rather concerned about what might happen after I finish writing both of my books. I certainly want to survive until I can see both of my books published, but what happens after that? I have told her that there are other books that I could write with regards to helping the Church to become ready for Christ's return. In fact, the Lord has already shown me what I should be writing about in my next book. This came through a couple of things that happened on a Sunday morning. One was what a speaker was saying on television and then God also told me about it in church.

I will always find ways to keep busy. I do want to serve Christ as long as I am alive on the earth, and after I go to be with Him, I still will want to serve Him with all of my heart. The main way for me to do that right now is for me to write books that bring Him glory and honor. I hope that this book will do that as well as my other book. God does deserve all of the glory that I can give Him. He alone is worthy!

I believe that God is going to heal me, but if He doesn't I can say that I am ready one-way or the other. I am certainly ready to be healed, but I am also ready if He wants to take me home. Actually though, if I am going to die, there are several plans that would have to be made. I expect that all plans with regards to my funeral should be made ahead of time, so that our family members would not have to make such decisions after my death. Those plans are partly made already because we have decided upon our graves in a graveyard already. We also have plans for the funeral including who will be in charge of it. I expect that additional planning will be completed quite soon.

Some people feel that if we have faith to believe that I am going to be healed, there is no need to make plans for a funeral or things like that. This is partly true, but it is still important to have such plans made because one day we will all die unless Christ returns first. I believe that my grandchildren and possibly my children will definitely be alive when Christ returns. There is no doubt in my mind about that. Christ's return to this earth is close at hand! His sudden return would then make all planning in our lives changed radically, wouldn't they? But the question is, how would we care if God changed our plans radically? I would love to see Him begin the plans that He has for the end of this Age of Grace that we are currently in.

All plans that we make are predicated upon the fact that I will not survive long if Christ does not heal me. I expect that He will heal me, but who can tell what plans He has for me? I certainly want to bring Him glory and I can do that whatever happens.

Reflections From My Wife

My husband and I started going together when I was fifteen years old and he was seventeen. We went together for three years and we married when I was eighteen and he was twenty. I guess you could say we have been together for most of our lives. We are young grandparents and I thought how we would be able to enjoy our grandchildren and they would remember us a being young and full of life. I pictured us when we were old as living and taking care of each other. My husband was only fifty-seven when this terrible disease came upon him. We have very blessed to always have a very close family, spending a lot of Sundays together.

We love to go for walks together. We would spend a lot of time talking about many things. When we found out about his A.L.S. we continued to go for the walks. We would talk about what could happen in the future and I would have my cry, and then we would resume our walk. We are thankful that Howard can still walk but things have changed. No longer were the walks a real time of communication but a time when we hold hands and look at the beautiful scenery that we see when we walk.

The day the new electric bed arrived was a day of mixed feelings for me. We had been in the same bed for almost 38 years. No longer would we be cuddling with his arm around me and my head laid on his shoulder, which we did every night before we went to sleep. This always gave me such a feeling of security. We have hardly ever been apart in those years. I had mixed emotions about this bed. On one hand I knew this bed meant that Howard would be able to sleep and breathe much better with the front of the bed elevated, but on the other hand he was leaving my bed probably forever unless God intervened.

We loved to go out to restaurants for many special occasions; Howard especially loved to go out for breakfast. With him having the feeding tube now he is not able to partake in this. After he came home with the feeding tube and we went to our daughter's place for the first time for a meal, I could hardly make myself eat. It was one of my favorite meals and yet I had to force it down. I felt so bad that I could eat and Howard could no longer have that enjoyment. I had no desire to make any food even for myself. We used to always have a lot of company over and I would make big meals. Now I can hardly stand to make any food.

When our youngest daughter moved in with us I finally forced myself to make some food. The prospect of making meals has gone from real enjoyment to hardly being able to make one. We had a gift of hospitality and now it seems to be gone or at least it has changed a lot. We still have people over but not as many. Instead of inviting them over for a big meal we invite them over for coffee. Our oldest daughter and her husband have a real gift for hospitality and they do a wonderful job at it. This has been a relief for me not to feel that we have to do it.

Through all the struggles, God has given us an inner peace that only He can give. It cannot be explained but only felt deep in our spirits. I know that God is in control of our lives, and I know that He knows what is best for us. I am learning to put my hand in His and to know that when times get too hard, He will pick us up in His arms and carry us through the situation. Yes there are days when I am only hanging on by a string but that string is connected to God. There are times when I tell God that the burdens are so heavy I can hardly manage. Then I am reminded of the scripture to give all burdens to Him and He will carry me through. *Cast your cares on the LORD and he will sustain you; he will never let the righteous fall.* (Psalm 55:22)

There is a song that I play daily. It states, "I have been through enough to know that He is enough for me." I can only manage to live one day at a time, which is what His Word tells us to do. I have to be thankful for each day that God gives to us and try to make the most of it. I hold onto the fact that God is in control of every day and He will only allow what I can handle for that day. I hold onto the 23rd Psalm:

> *The LORD is my shepherd, I shall not be in want. He makes me lie down in green pastures, He leads me beside quiet waters, He restores my soul. He guides me in paths of righteousness for His name's sake. Even though I walk through the valley of the shadow of death, I will fear no evil, for You are with me; Your rod and Your staff, they comfort me. You prepare a table before me in the presence of my enemies. You anoint my head with oil; my cup overflows. Surely goodness and love will follow me all the days of my life, and I will dwell in the house of the LORD forever.*

As we continue to go through these trials and tests I know that we are never alone because God is always with us. I marvel at the beautiful spirit my husband has had through all of this. With all that he has gone through there has only been a few times that there has been a hint of discouragement. As I watch the A.L.S. taking over and his body failing him, I am seeing that his spirit has grown stronger with each trial. I have always loved my husband but as I watch how he is going through this without complaining, I have grown to love him even more deeply than before. As a caregiver, he has made my life so much easier because of his consistency. I know things are hard for him since he has lost his ability to do so many things that he did before, yet his spirit man is so very strong.

There is something else that I wanted to share with you. It is hard for me to see my husband going through all of this. I know that he is having a hard time. He tells people that if God is not going to heal him he would like to go home. I love him very much and I don't know what I would do if God decides to take him home. But on the other hand I love him too much so that I don't want him to suffer. He has suffered a lot. I have to think of him and not myself. He says his body is failing but his spirit is strong. I know that God can heal him without a doubt. I also know that he has gone through so much without complaining. It is hard to watch someone you love go down hill. The changes have been so great. I do not know what each day will hold but I do know who holds tomorrow and I know He holds my hand. I am not feeling depressed. We have to just look at each day and be thankful for that day.

Many people say how strong I am and I know that it is not my own strength. I really believe that my strength comes from the prayers of the people from all over the world. I want to thank everyone who has been and is still praying for us. I know that it is the prayers of God's people who have helped us to walk through this valley. I believe that prayer is the most important thing you can do to help someone in their time of need. God hears the prayers and gives us strength for the day. I can really feel when there are many people praying because it becomes like a prayer covering over us and we seem to get extra strength.

***

I really do thank God for Ann. She has been a strong support for me, and I value the thoughts that she has given me about this book. By the way, she was the first one who felt that I should write this book. She was thinking that I could be a help to others who are going through similar trials. I know that this time is extremely difficult for her, but I also know that God has been her strength.

A Continuous Desire to Serve Christ

One of the most difficult problems is due to the fact that I can no longer speak. I would love to be able to do so because I do have a burden in my heart for believers who are living close to the world instead of living for Christ. On the eve of His coming, I feel it is very important for the Church to become ready for His return. The only avenue I have now for that is to write. It is my hope that believers who read my books might catch the same vision that I have.

Ever since I found Christ as my Saviour I have wanted to serve Him with all of my heart. If I look back on my life (which I do quite a bit these days) there certainly were times in which I have fallen short of living for Him. As most people have, there are times when we forget about our need to be of service to God instead of to ourselves. That unfortunately is the big problem for many Christians.

It is quite different, however, when you have a terminal disease. I want to serve Him with all of my heart because I definitely want to bring honor to Him. I hope that my life has done that to a certain extent. Now I can only hope that my attitude with this disease might point others to Jesus Christ because it is our God Who is helping me to have a positive outlook for the future. Also of course, if God is going to take me home to be with Him, it is my hope that He will notice what I am doing during my last days to minister to Him.

We have a great and powerful God, and it is my desire for all believers to recognize God's goodness in everything that takes place in our lives. He is always with us, no matter what situation we are going through. I would like all believers to realize that God wants to use them, no matter what situation they are in. I believe that this is our responsibility and I feel that all who know Christ as their Saviour should be looking at ways in which they can serve Him.

Christ expects all of us to fulfill the Great Commission that He gave to us. There are many Christians who feel the Great Commission doesn't apply to them, but it certainly does. That doesn't mean that all of us should become missionaries or pastors, but it still means that we should have a ministry that reaches out to others. Following is the Great Commission that God wants all of us to be active participants in.

> *Then Jesus came to them and said, "All authority in heaven and on earth has been given to Me. Therefore go and make disciples of all nations, baptizing them in the name of the Father and of the Son and of the Holy Spirit, and teaching them to obey everything I have commanded you. And surely I am with you always, to the very end of the age."*
> (Matthew 28:18 – 20)

I have tried to follow God's will for my life in a couple of avenues for ministry: 1) Creating and administrating Christian schools and, 2) pastoring in churches as well as teaching in a Bible College. However, I am not satisfied with what I have accomplished. I still would like to do more for God. Writing might be another avenue of serving Him, but He will have to help me to make the books that I write into something that is popular as well as life changing for people. I have to rely on God for doing that.

You see, God has placed a real burden in my heart – that is to reach out to all Christians and try to motivate them to work for God in some way or another. Do you realize that only about twenty-five percent of all Christians ever work in a church no matter how big that church is? Ministering to God in churches goes far beyond what a pastor does. God uses individuals as Sunday school teachers, to serve on boards, to drive carloads of teens to a special activity, and many more ministries. Notice that there are many ministries within a church that you can get involved with. Please note that a person who is mature enough to be a board member should have already been involved in some type of ministry and has proven himself\herself as being faithful to God's calling in his\her life. If you are really ready to serve God, I hope you are involved in a Bible-believing church and that you are ready to volunteer to help someone with their ministry. May God speak to the hearts of His people and guide them into being able to minister to others.

God really does want all of His followers to become busy for Him in relation to building His kingdom. We are to be building His kingdom regularly by leading people to Christ or working to create more disciples for Him. As we anticipate Christ's soon return it would be good to see all of His followers busily working in His Kingdom so that many more would be ready for His coming.

Peter wrote some important thoughts, which are directed at believers who are unsure about God's call upon their lives. *"Therefore, my brothers, be all the more eager to make your calling and election sure. For if you do these things, you will never fall, and you will receive a rich welcome into the eternal kingdom of our Lord and Saviour Jesus Christ."* (2 Peter 1:10,11) You can see that God has called each Christian to become part of His family. It is important that you even attend a church that you feel God has called you to. He also has called you to become active in His kingdom in order to receive that "rich welcome" into His glory. But believe me that if you become active in His kingdom now, you also will receive a "rich welcome" from the people that you are helping. You will find that God will have a rich blessing for you if you do become a worker in His kingdom.

Having a Terminal Disease but No Hope

I would like to address those who may read this book but don't yet know Jesus Christ as their Saviour. If you are suffering from a fatal disease, my heart goes out to you, because I am in the same condition as you are. I don't know how advanced you might be as far as your disease is concerned, but I don't know how much time I have left myself. It all depends how quickly the disease will move into my lungs. It seems that it is there already, but I still have a good content of oxygen in my blood, so that is good. I realize that my time could be very limited, but no one can predict when the end might come.

What kind of condition are you in? If you are in the last stages of your disease, it means that you don't have very much time left. If you are without Jesus Christ as your Saviour, you will have nothing to look forward to. However, if you have read this book, you can definitely see that I have a tremendous amount of hope. In fact it is difficult for me to ask God to heal me, because I know the glories that will await me in the future. If you give your heart to Jesus Christ, He will change your life completely. Suddenly you will be full of hope and you can find victory in your spirit even if your body is failing you.

Eternity is much greater than living for sixty years. I have a body that I would not want to live for 20 more years in, if God does not heal me. I would rather that He would take me home.

You might not be in a condition to say that, but I certainly do encourage you to repent of your sins and ask Jesus to come into your heart. This will change your heart and your spirit forever.

I realize that your background might make this very difficult for you. You may be in a position whereby your family might disown you if you accept Christ. I realize that this could be very difficult for you, but I encourage you to do this anyway. In some religions there is no hope for what will come after you die. I hope you are not in a position where you have to wait for the death angel to take you to heaven or hell. This is not Biblical, and I do encourage you to read the Bible, because this is the greatest testimony of truth that you will find anywhere.

You may be a person who does not follow any religion and have never had anything to do with a church in your past. All of a sudden you developed a disease that you know very little about. You may also be a person who does not have much support from your family or your friends. That would make you very lonely and without hope, particularly if you have A.L.S. because there is absolutely no cure for this disease.

The only hope for recovery that I have is God healing me. I personally have more hope in the future because I know that God has prepared a place for me to live in His glory! That does not mean that I don't have hope for healing, because I do. God is well able to heal me if He wants to. He could snap His fingers and I would be instantly healed!

In your situation, I would truly ask you to come to Jesus because He can change your life and your circumstances completely. Where you previously had little or no hope, He can give you hope that will never leave you, as long as you follow Him for the rest of you life. Now is the time to call on His name and seek His power in your body. He will respond, and you will be changed completely. If you are well enough to go to church I encourage you to go to a Bible-believing church as regularly as you can.

If you cannot go to church, I encourage you to read the Bible each day, probably starting with the Book of John. I also encourage you to watch television programs where the Word of God is being preached. These messages would help you, though you should contact a Bible-believing church in your neighbourhood so that people from the church could come and visit you on a regular basis. God wants to reach out to you in your time of distress. May He help you in your time of suffering and despair. Understand please that God loves you, no matter what your background might be. He loves everyone regardless if they do not return His love.

A Word to Caregivers

I want to take the time to thank all caregivers of people who have a terminal disease. You are invaluable to us who are suffering such a disease. The caregivers that I have are certainly the most important people that I have – mostly my family but also several professional people – both through home care and those associated with the A.L.S. Clinic that is run in our location.

The work that you are doing is a very important when you can help the victims to become as comfortable as possible. May God richly bless you for your assistance!

As you can see from earlier in this chapter, my wife is the best caregiver that I have. Spouses can become that for terminal patients. I realize that some of you might be just like some of the victims that I was speaking to recently in this chapter. You could be caregivers without any hope at all for your loved one, and as a result you might become pretty tired and worn out.

I would really like you to take time to consider what I written in this book about a hope that you would have if you too would accept Christ as your Saviour. It would be great if you and the loved one you are caring about decided together to accept Christ as your Saviour. This would indeed revolutionize your home and would make dying not quite as difficult to face.

It is true that you would certainly miss your loved one, just as I know that if I die my loved ones would miss me quite a bit. However, they would also be comforted by the fact that they would probably see me some day in heaven.

There is no bigger step that you could take than for you and your loved one accepting Christ as your Saviour. All of a sudden your lives would be changed and transformed. Then you would not be living for yourself but living for God. Allow Him to come into your hearts so that He could help you to face any burden that you might have in the future.

Right now your work with your loved one is precious. No one could replace the work that you are doing. God bless you as you work to help the victim of a fatal disease.

A Final Word to All

I have talked to you a great deal about my condition and about the thoughts that I have had regarding this disease that will take my life unless God intervenes. You know my thoughts and how God has helped me with regards to this disease. I want everyone to know that I depend upon my God each day to give me the strength I need to walk through this hardship that I am having. I want you to know that I am very grateful to God one way or another – if I die or if I live. As I stated earlier, I will be blessed one way or another - if I die or if I am healed.

If I am healed I expect to be able to go to several public meetings to tell others about what God has done for me. Therefore I would expect that many of you would hear about God healing me. Likewise, I expect by emails that you will hear if I die with this affliction. Please remember that with me death has no sting or victory! My victory is in Jesus Christ my Lord. I am very pleased to give Him all the honour that I can through this book, as well as through other books that I am writing.

I am asking everyone who reads this book to take a look at your spiritual condition. Are you living for God or for yourself? If you are a Christian and living for yourself, you need to repent and allow Christ to become Lord of your life! If you are not a Christian, I encourage you to accept Him as your Saviour and repent of the dead works that you have been involved in. Read the Bible and begin attending a Bible – believing church so that God can use you in these last days.

God bless each one who has read this book!